"The way that—in this social and political climate—Harold Heie believes it might just be possible to have 'respectful conversations' in which 'listening well' prevails must make him the Don Quixote of the Christian world. But maybe, instead of being lost in a never-never land of impossibility, Harold is actually walking the narrow path that leads to eternal life. Read the book to find out why that outrageous idea might actually be the truth."

—MARK NOLL
Author of *Jesus Christ and the Life of the Mind*

"Thanks to Harold Heie for his new book, *Let's Talk*. God knows how much we need it in these divisive times! If you'd like to be part of the solution rather than just complaining about the problem, this is a timely, helpful resource."

—BRIAN D. MCLAREN
Author of *Faith after Doubt: Why Your Beliefs Stopped Working and What to Do about It*

"In this revealing and compelling memoir, Heie demonstrates the many qualities that set him apart as a mature and exemplary follower of Jesus. For years, Heie has been calling us to what he calls 'respectful conversations,' marked by the biblical characteristics of 'gentleness and respect.' Those qualities, together with the author's characteristic humility, make this a book worthy of serious consideration."

—RANDALL BALMER
Dartmouth College

LET'S TALK

LET'S TALK

*Bridging Divisive Lines through Inclusive
and Respectful Conversations*

HAROLD HEIE

Foreword by Richard J. Mouw
Afterwords by David P. Gushee
and Stan D. Gaede

CASCADE *Books* · Eugene, Oregon

LET'S TALK
Bridging Divisive Lines through Inclusive and Respectful Conversations

Cascade Books
An Imprint of Wipf and Stock Publishers
199 W. 8th Ave., Suite 3
Eugene, OR 97401

www.wipfandstock.com

PAPERBACK ISBN: 978-1-7252-9605-3
HARDCOVER ISBN: 978-1-7252-9606-0
EBOOK ISBN: 978-1-7252-9607-7

Cataloguing-in-Publication data:

Names: Heie, Harold.

Title: Let's Talk: Bridging Divisive Lines through Inclusive and Respectful Conversations / Harold Heie.

Description: Eugene, OR: Cascade Books, 2021 | Series: if applicable | Includes bibliographical references.

Identifiers: ISBN 978-1-7252-9605-3 (paperback) | ISBN 978-1-7252-9606-0 (hardcover) | ISBN 978-1-7252-9607-7 (ebook)

Subjects: LCSH: Polarization—United States. | Political participation—Moral and ethical aspects—United States.

Classification: call number BV4647.C78 H47 2021 (paperback) | call number BV4647 (ebook)

12/09/21

Dedicated to my mentors, with deep appreciation for the splendid ways in which they broadened my understanding of what it means to be a follower of Jesus

Prayer of Confession

God, we believe you have called us to unity
Forgive us for the times we have chosen isolation over relationship with those who are different from us
God, we believe you have called us to live together as one body
Forgive us for the times we have created division and encouraged disunity within your church
God, we believe you ask us to look, listen, and learn from others as those created in your image
Forgive us for the times we have ridiculed and attacked those with different viewpoints, failing to love others as we love ourselves

AMERICAN REFORMED CHURCH
Orange City, Iowa
January 19, 2020

Contents

Foreword

If twenty years ago I had come across a book on respectful conversations, I would have thought: What a good topic. We need more conversations that exhibit mutual respect.

These days, though, I see the topic as addressing a desperate need. Indeed, in our present cultural context, the notion of engaging in respectful conversations smacks of utopianism. Disrespect has almost become the norm in our collective discourse. It abounds in the halls of national leadership, on the internet and cable television, in the aisles of Walmart stores, and, increasingly, even on university campuses.

In the midst of all of this there are, of course, many folks—including many Christian folks—who are looking for ways to facilitate positive change. I, for one, welcome the effort by anyone who wants to offer remedies. I greet the publication of this book by Harold Heie, however, with more than a warm welcome. It is an occasion for joy. Harold not only brings much clear thinking to the subject of respectful conversation, but he also bears the marks of a respectful conversationalist in his own person in admirable ways.

There is much wisdom to be found in these pages. Harold has a scholar's grasp of the key issues. As a Christian thinker, for example, he shows us how to mine diverse—and, some would say, irreconcilable—theological traditions for a solid grasp of what must go into an integrated faith-based understanding of civil discourse. And he does this by drawing upon lessons learned in his own personal journey, having been shaped at different stages by Lutheran pietism, Reformed worldview thinking, and an Anabaptist conception of discipleship.

Harold also shares the pain he experienced when he was summarily dismissed from a position in which he thought he was flourishing as leader. In an impressive manner, he tells the story without indulging in self-pity, with the result that the episode actually serves to highlight the points he wants to make about the importance of listening and learning in cultivating a respectful spirit.

It is precisely this kind of personal candor that infuses his overall discussion with the practical character that is often missing in studies of civil discourse. Harold not only offers counsel about how to initiate and guide conversations in which people engage each other regarding matters where they deeply disagree, but he also gives us real case studies from his own efforts.

The stories of his convening local groups, particularly in congregations, to work at respectful conversation is not a narrative about astounding successes. Rather, we learn from what he has learned when things went badly, as well as from when he experienced promising outcomes.

A prominent theme in these pages is what Harold describes as "planting tiny seeds of redemption." I came to love that image as I read this book. The major work of redemption has, of course, been accomplished through what God has done for us in Jesus Christ. As disciples of Jesus, we encounter huge challenges in our present world. But we do not have to take on all of the sins of the world. That has already been done by an all-sufficient Savior. Our task is to take on what we can realistically expect to accomplish in the contexts where the Lord has called us to serve. Planting tiny seeds is important Christian work.

Harold Heie does not claim to have produced a great harvest of respectful conversations. But he does show us what it is like to plant the seeds. In this wonderful book, he has planted some important seeds in my own mind and heart. May it be the same for all who listen and learn from the wisdom he shares in these pages!

Richard J. Mouw

Acknowledgments

In many ways this is a rather unusual book, especially in its attempt to build bridges between areas of discourse that are usually segregated—most notably, I attempt to forge connections between narratives that may appeal to a popular audience (the many personal anecdotes about the influence of my most significant mentors) and some scholarly reflections that may appeal to Christians working in the academy.

To continue that theme, my acknowledgments will first attempt to build a bridge between two areas that are too often separated: books and people.

As a kid in Brooklyn, I was not one of those precocious readers who made regular trips to the local library. I didn't even know the location of my local library. I only read what my teachers assigned for me to read, nothing less and nothing more. I much preferred to spend my spare time playing stickball[1] on the street on which I lived in the Bay Ridge section of Brooklyn (56th Street, between 7th and 8th Avenues).

I became a voracious reader only after earning my doctorate, belatedly realizing that what I could read in books could richly inform my attempts to live well. Reading books has been a passion of

---

1. Stickball is like baseball, but it uses a rubber ball filled with air and a broomstick without the broom. Home plate and second base are steel-covered entries to the sewer below, thirty yards apart. First base and third base are doors on the driver's side of parked cars. One's ability as a stickball player was measured by how far one could hit the ball. I was only a two-sewer guy (a mere 180 feet). Wille Mays and Yankees star Joe Pepitone were reported to be three-sewer guys, which is awesome.

mine ever since I came to that life-changing realization. (There are few things that give me more pleasure than curling up with a good book in my office at home.)

But as much as what I have read in books has helped me in my attempts to live well as I aspire to be a faithful follower of Jesus, it has been the modeling of such faithfulness by other people (most notably, my mentors) that has had the most formative influence on me (mentorship not divorced from the reading of good books but complementing such reading, since many of my mentors have pointed me to the good books I have read).

All of the above is to say that my first acknowledgment as I conclude this book is to express thankfulness to all my mentors and all the other persons I name in this book, all of whom have had a profound influence on my attempt to live well as a follower of Jesus. Their influence on me permeates the content of this book.

But there are other persons, most of whom I have not mentioned by name in this book, whom I wish to specifically acknowledge at this time.

I want to thank the seventy-five "conversation partners" who have generously contributed to my various attempts to orchestrate respectful conversations (online and in person) about contentious issues these past ten years. They are too numerous for me to mention them by name here; the interested reader can identify them by going to my website.

I want to thank Estee Zandee, who served with distinction as an editorial assistant and publishing consultant for this book. Her insights into what makes for compelling writing and her ability to help me to greatly improve upon earlier drafts of this book were nothing short of extraordinary.

I want to thank Richard Mouw for writing the foreword. Richard has been my hero for many years as a pioneer in orchestrating respectful conversations about contentious issues. It is an honor and source of great encouragement to have a Christian statesman of his stature and sterling reputation express appreciation for this book.

I want to thank David Gushee for writing an afterword. David has been a strong supporter of my respectful conversation initiatives over many years, for which I am most appreciative. He has also modeled for me that rare combination of commitment to one's beliefs and openness to the possibility of modifying one's beliefs as a result of listening carefully to the contrary beliefs of others.

I also wish to thank Stan Gaede for writing a concluding afterword. Stan has been a dear friend of mine for forty-five years, and knows who I am, both professionally and personally, better than anyone I know outside of my immediate family. Since a major theme of this book is that people's beliefs about any issue should flow from and comport with who they are, I deeply appreciate Stan's willingness to reflect on that integral connection in my life.

I also want to thank those who have written generous endorsements for this book: Mark Noll, Randall Balmer, John Wilson, Wesley Granberg-Michaelson, Elizabeth Brown Hardeman, and Brian McLaren. Each in his or her own way has helped me immensely during various stages of my pilgrimage, for which I am deeply appreciative.

I also wish to thank Rob Barrett, formerly with The Colossian Forum, who has been a true kindred spirit as we have attempted to orchestrate respectful conversations about contentious issues in differing, albeit complementary, ways in our respective spheres of influence. The many emails and telephone calls we have shared over recent years have been a constant source of encouragement, inspiration, and, yes, challenge.

I also thank Tamara Fynaardt for her careful reading of an original draft of this manuscript and her many very helpful suggestions for rewording. As she has often done for me in the past, Tamara helped me to write more clearly and succinctly.

I thank the many staff members at Wipf and Stock publishers for their fine work in bringing this book to the published light of day. I especially thank Rebecca Abbott for her splendid work copyediting a penultimate draft of my manuscript. Her meticulous attention to detail, her patience, and her kind spirit were truly remarkable. Likewise, I wish to thank Savanah N. Landerholm for her prompt and excellent typesetting work.

Finally, I want to thank those who have rescued me from my being a techno-bozo when it comes to matters pertaining to

Acknowledgments

websites. Many years ago, my good friend Christina Wassell from Massachusetts first encouraged me and then helped me to set up my website, for which I am most appreciative.

Since then, Dan Hefferan and Brian Workman have done extraordinary work managing my website, first with the Five Espressos website company, and then with Dauntless Digital, where Dan continued the management. My work these past ten years would not have been possible without their splendid assistance.

Introduction: Some Christian Virtues Are Foundational

I was emerging as a Christian big shot during my early days teaching mathematics at The King's College in Briarcliff Manor, New York. Or at least that is what I thought at the time.

In addition to my teaching responsibilities, for which I received laudatory evaluations from both my students and faculty peers, I was heavily involved in important institutional service assignments.

I also had the opportunity to speak at a few of the daily chapel services at TKC, after which it was not unusual for someone to say "Nice talk, Harold."

My sense of self-importance came to a grinding halt one evening next to the bathtub in our apartment as I bathed our three Js (Jonathan, Janice, and Jeffrey) prior to dinner. Our Js were unusually rambunctious that evening, and soon there was more water on the floor and me than was left in the bathtub.

Rather than joining in the fun, I lost my cool, yelling at my kids. That seemingly trivial incident in my life took on immense importance. Soaked from head to toe and hollering at my kids, I had a life-changing thought: my colleagues at TKC—whom I had fooled into thinking that I was a Christian big shot—should see me now.

The false start I had made in my attempts to follow Jesus reflects the erroneous view that my fidelity to Christ should be measured by my behavior in public. I realized the better measure was the kind of person I was when no one was around to applaud me—no one was around to say "Nice bath, Harold."

As a result of this apparently mundane experience, the biblical teaching about some foundational Christian virtues (what Galatians 5:22–23 calls the "fruit of the Spirit") became central to my understanding of how I should seek to follow Jesus. Whatever I am doing, wherever I am, whether or not there is anyone around to see, I ought to exemplify love, joy, peace, patience, kindness, generosity, faithfulness, gentleness, and self-control. That understanding has been a fixed point in my evolving beliefs about what it means to follow Jesus.

Since that moment next to the bathtub many years ago, I have aspired to be a person who exhibits fruit of the Spirit whether anyone is noticing or not. Although I have often failed to measure up to that ideal, I know for sure that it is the ideal. And the person who has most consistently modeled that ideal for me is my wife.

Meet Pat

I have never seen Pat, my wife of fifty-nine years, do anything to draw attention to herself, as she cares deeply for her family and friends in countless unassuming, behind-the-scenes ways. Pat will be the first to confess that she has not lived up to the ideals of the fruit of the Spirit perfectly. But she has mentored me in the routine humdrum of daily life, remarkably and consistently exemplifying love, joy, peace, patience, kindness, generosity, faithfulness, gentleness, and self-control. What is her motivation? It is because she believes, as I now do, that this is the kind of person that followers of Jesus are called to be. And, as I will report later, that calling is invariable, independent of whether the actions that emerge from being that kind of person can be judged to be successful.

The profound way in which Pat has been a mentor to me illustrates a truth about the nature of listening to others: listening is not done just with the ears; it is also done with the eyes. Pat has never preached to me about the centrality of the fruit of the Spirit. The way she lives speaks more loudly than any words possibly can.

The reason the fruit of the Spirit is foundational is that our attitudes (our enduring dispositions) deeply inform what we see needs to be done or said.

Consider first the general example portrayed in the story of the good Samaritan (Luke 10:25–37). The priest and the Levite who passed by the wounded man lying in a ditch were characterized by an attitude of indifference, which is the opposite of love. The good Samaritan, characterized by attitudes of compassion and love, stopped to help the wounded man. Being characterized by the fruit of the Spirit will help you to know what to do, which is a cardinal feature of the dynamism of Christian living. As you live faithful to your current understanding of what it means to follow Jesus, you gain greater understanding about how you should continue following.

Consider also the more specific example of trying to orchestrate inclusive respectful conversations across dividing lines. The common practice of shutting down a political conversation by means of a strident expression of your current beliefs accompanied by demonization of those who disagree with you is antithetical to Christian teachings.

The Christian approach for orchestrating inclusive respectful conversations across dividing lines starts with creating a safe and welcoming space for the person who disagrees with you, followed by careful listening as a deep expression of love. This book will elaborate on this Christian way of engaging someone who disagrees with you.

CHAPTER 1

Major Obstacles to Inclusive and Respectful Conversations, with the Essential First Step

It is indisputable that the current state of public discourse is deplorable. When people disagree about contentious issues, they too easily resort to name-calling and demonization of the other without any serious attempt to find common ground by means of respectful conversations about their disagreements.

This brokenness in public discourse is not limited to any one segment of the population. It can be seen when Christians vilify one another because of different beliefs regarding human sexuality. It breaks out when secularists and people holding to a variety of religious beliefs demonize one another because of differing political affiliations and convictions.

Since I travel most frequently in Christian circles, this book will focus on identifying problems and proposing solutions to the vitriolic engagements that Christians too often have with other Christians about their disagreements. But it will soon become apparent that the values that underlie my proposed solutions are not just Christian values; they are human values that all people of good will should embrace, whatever their worldview or beliefs.

Based on the above reflections, it is important for me to be clear about the purpose of this book. It is *not* to resolve disagreements about select contentious issues. Rather, in light of the highly polarized and divided nature of contemporary American culture, the purpose of this book is to provide practical, actionable suggestions for bridging divisions—even in the face of significant disagreement—through respectful conversation. Such respectful engagement could lead to uncovering some common ground. But whether it does or not, I will propose that it is the right thing to do based on the Christian values to which I am committed.

In brief, it is my hope that any reader will discover in these pages ways to navigate difficult yet important conversations by cultivating safe and loving communities that practice inclusive respectful conversations.

My Story in Just a Few Words

Love for others creates a safe and welcoming space to talk respectfully about disagreements.

Arthur Brooks has proposed that a good way to "start telling your story" is to "write it down in twelve words or less."[1] I overshot his suggestion by two words.

Where My Story Begins

I made a commitment to the Christian faith at the age of thirteen, in the basement of the Norwegian Evangelical Lutheran Free Church in Brooklyn, New York (Fifty-Ninth Street Church to us teenagers).

What stands out most in my memory of that decision is an intense realization of being unconditionally loved by God through Jesus Christ, and a compulsion to express my gratitude for such unmerited love by making a commitment to Christianity.

But at that tender age, I had little understanding of what such a commitment to the Christian faith really means. I understood little of the lifelong implications. In particular, I didn't have a clue as to the many twists and turns that my Christian pilgrimage would take. And I had absolutely no idea of the vast diversity of understanding among Christians down through the ages about what it means

1. Brooks, *Love Your Enemies*, 151.

to be a Christian. Does it involve obedience to the two great love commandments from Jesus ("Love the Lord your God with all your heart and with all your soul and with all your mind. . . . And love your neighbor as yourself" Matt 22:36–40)? Does it involve adherence to one or more of the historic Christian creeds? Does it involve embracing a particular set of essentials of the Christian faith, some short and some very long, as formulated by a given Christian tradition, denomination, or organization?

Situating Myself as a Follower of Jesus

My present response when I am asked about my most fundamental identity is that I aspire to be a follower of Jesus. I am content with this self-designation because of the biblical teaching that God wishes for those who profess to be Christians to be transformed into the "likeness of Christ" (2 Cor 3:18; 5:17).

As the narrative that follows will reveal—starting with my boyhood days in Brooklyn and culminating in my extensive experience these past ten years orchestrating respectful conversations among Christians who have strong disagreements—a central facet of my understanding of what it means to follow Jesus is that I need to create safe and welcoming spaces for the expression of disagreements as a deep expression of the love for others to which Jesus calls all who claim to be his followers.

But I am sure that many readers would like me to say still more about my understanding of what it means to be a follower of Jesus. So here are a few more words of elaboration: I personally trust in Jesus Christ as essential for my salvation and for the redemption of the entire created order, and I aspire to follow Jesus by being obedient to the two great love commandments taught by Jesus: love for God and love for neighbor.

It is important for me to point out what my minimalist profession does not say. It does not assert a particular theory of atonement (how Jesus Christ is essential for my salvation and for the redemption of the entire created order). It says nothing about origins (how God created the cosmos). It says nothing about eschatology (the manner in which the kingdom of God will one day be fully realized). It says nothing about the nature of the Trinity (that God is one person in three persons). It says nothing about my position or posture on hot-button social issues (e.g., same-sex marriage or political affiliation).

But I recognize that other Christians are committed to different elaborations—possibly wanting to say much more about what following Jesus entails, including an appeal to one or more of the historic Christian creeds, or commitment to a particular set of essentials of the Christian faith.

So, in light of this great diversity amongst Christians about the essentials of what it means to be a follower of Jesus, how can Christians flourish together in the midst of their differing views about what is truly essential? My radical proposal is this: *Let us embrace, as brothers and sisters in Christ, all who aspire to be followers of Jesus, allowing for a diversity of beliefs about what it means to follow Jesus.*[2]

Therefore, my first primary audience for this book is comprised of those Christians who are committed to following Jesus, as they understand the meaning of that commitment, and who allow for a diversity of Christ-follower essentials among other Christians.

But if you are a Christian, an important precondition is necessary. This book can be your guide for navigating difficult yet important conversations and cultivating safe and loving communities only if you embrace both *commitment* to your present beliefs about what it means to be a follower of Jesus and *openness* to carefully considering the contrary beliefs of other Christ followers—an openness that could lead to a refinement, or even correction, of your present beliefs.

---

2. This proposal comports with the spirit of the recent work of some theologians who propose a paradigm for doing theology that calls for a "centered-set" of Christian beliefs rather than a "bounded-set." This paradigm suggests that the current preoccupation with establishing firm boundaries to decide who is inside and who is outside the Christian fold should be replaced by asking who is nearer the center and who is moving away from it. For those who accept this way of thinking about doing theology, I would propose that the center can be viewed as the aspiration to be a follower of Jesus. For further elaboration, see Olson, *Reformed and Always Reforming,* 53–65.

I believe exemplifying this rare alchemy of commitment and openness will enrich your life by combining the importance of living true to your present convictions with the importance of always seeking greater understanding. And this enrichment is possible for all human beings, not just Christians.

The Essential First Step for Engaging Christians (and Others) Who Disagree with You: Listening Well

We were Lutheran kids from Brooklyn. Our theological instruction was limited to memorizing Luther's *Small Catechism* for confirmation. No attempts were made in our Sunday school instruction to introduce us to the beliefs of Christians in other Protestant traditions who held beliefs that differed from the tenets of Lutheranism. And our Roman Catholic neighbors were certainly beyond the pale, since their "works righteousness" violated the Lutheran distinction between law and gospel (or, at least, that is what we were led to believe). And the Orthodox branch of Christianity was not even on our radar.

As will eventually become apparent, although I heartily embrace certain aspects of my Lutheran upbringing, my current theological beliefs, which slowly emerged as I engaged in more inclusive conversations, now place me in the Reformed/Anabaptist category (with all the tensions that arise from this unusual combination; more about that later). How did this happen?

This happened because of my exposure to theological otherness. As my successive involvement in various inclusive conversations exposed me to deeply committed believers who worshipped in other Christian traditions (especially some of my mentors), I was exposed to beliefs about what it means to be a follower of Jesus that differed from some major tenets of Lutheranism.

Of course, I could have dismissed these alternative Christian beliefs out of hand. But I listened. Why? Because I soon discovered that these new Christian friends aspired as much as I did to be faithful followers of Jesus, and the commendable ways in which they gave evidence of Christlikeness led me to conclude that I had much to learn from carefully listening to them.

Five Major Obstacles to Creating Safe and Welcoming Spaces for Listening Well

#1: Denying Diversity of Christian Beliefs

One major obstacle to the message of this book is the denial of diversity in Christian beliefs that considers "manyness" to be a failure.

Diversity in Christian belief has been prominent since the early days of the Christian church, and it is here to stay. Many Christian historians have documented this truth.[3] Catherine Brekus and Clark Gilpin have cogently pointed out the problem:

> Christians usually identify "manyness" as a failure. Christians believe that in the ideal world, the tradition is supposed to be singular, and rather than confronting its plurality, they have usually chosen to identify their own part of it with the whole.[4]

#2: Tribalism

The tendency of many Christians to perceive "manyness" as a failure cannot be overstated. It is a symptom of the extent to which many Christians have succumbed to the tribalism that is the scourge of public discourse in our day. The essence of tribalism is an us-versus-them mentality that holds that "me and my people"—whether my church, my denomination, or my Christian tradition—have the truth, the whole truth, and nothing but the truth regarding Christian belief and practice, and those "other folks" possess very little, if any, of that truth.[5] This tribalism becomes particularly pernicious

3. Two of the most compelling accounts I have read are Brekus and Gilpin, *American Christianities*, and Evans, *Histories*.

4. Brekus and Gilpin, *American Christianities*, 4.

5. The scourge of tribalism is an aberration of a valuable aspect of being human: the importance of being a member of one or more communities (tribes)

when an unwarranted leap is made from "you are wrong" to "you are an evil person who should be demonized." As David French points out, the starting point for overcoming such tribalism is to embrace a view of tolerance as showing "kindness and respect toward people who are not of *your* group."[6] Unfortunately, for those who embrace tribalism, "Kindness is perceived as weakness. Decency is treated as if it's cowardness. Acts of grace are an unthinkable concession to evil."[7] How then, does one seek to overcome such tribalism? French suggests that one must model a better way: "Be prepared to model tolerance and grace even as you keep to your underlying principles and convictions."[8]

#3: Rejecting the Rare Combination of Commitment and Openness in Conversation

The better way French advises rarely happens. Those Christians who believe that their tribe has singular insight into all of God's truth will have little incentive to combine such strong commitment with an openness to respectfully engage in conversation with those who disagree with them. Richard Mouw, president emeritus of Fuller Theological Seminary, points to the rarity of this combination among Christians in a fascinating (and disturbing) reflection on the many sermons he heard on the last two sentences in 1 Peter 3:15 during his boyhood days in a Christian Reformed church in New Jersey.

> Always be prepared to give an answer to everyone who asks you to give the reason for the hope that you have. But do this with gentleness and respect. (NIV)

Mouw observes that he heard many sermons on the first sentence, but he has no recollection of ever having heard a sermon on the second.

---

of persons who care for one another, providing a clear sense of belonging and solidarity. For a splendid account of this positive aspect of being a member of a tribe, see Junger, *Tribe*.

6. French, *Divided We Fall*, 106 (emphasis original).

7. French, *Divided We Fall*, 253.

8. French, *Divided We Fall*, 252.

This radical example of the penchant of many Christians to hear and repeat biblical passages out of their context (within the same verse, mind you) points to the rarity of this combination of commitment and openness. Here is my own elaboration.

The first sentence from 1 Peter 3:15 suggests that Christians should be prepared to state their beliefs with clarity and conviction. That reflects strong commitment to one's Christian beliefs. So far, so good! But the oft-neglected second sentence suggests how a Christian should state her strong convictions: with "gentleness and respect." For me this exhortation to be gentle and respectful means that as you state your Christian beliefs with clarity and conviction, at the same time you are also open to listening to and seriously considering the contrary beliefs of others and then talking respectfully about your agreements and disagreements. The mistake of Christians who practice tribalism is to embrace commitment but to eschew openness. The rarity of this combination of commitment and openness is the main obstacle to Christians embracing and learning from the diversity in their beliefs.

Based on his extensive experience engaging in interfaith dialogues with Catholics, Jews, and Mormons, Mouw has provided excellent advice for how to signal to your conversation partners your openness to listening and giving serious consideration to their contrary viewpoints as a first step in bridging any divides. He used to jump right into the fray, telling the other person in no uncertain terms why she was wrong, which led only to defensiveness. Now he starts by saying to the other person, "Help me to understand what it is you believe [about the issue at hand] and your reasons for believing that."

Mouw found that this way of starting the conversation "softens the heart." As the writer of Proverbs says, "A soft answer turns away wrath" (15:1).

As you will eventually read, I have some firsthand experience proving the wisdom of first listening well in order to adequately understand the contrary beliefs of others before seeking to sort through areas of agreement and disagreement. It is wise because when the other person realizes you are genuinely interested in understanding what she believes and why she holds to those beliefs, she will often reciprocate, leading to the quest for mutual under-standing. Listening well also leads to the trust that is a necessary foundation for sorting through disagreements in the hope of find-ing some common ground. Or, if that doesn't happen, trust at least enables ongoing conversation.

#4: Posing False Either/Or Choices in Conversation

I remember well the belated going-away party that the faculty at Messiah College threw for me in 1994, about eighteen months after I left my position as vice president for academic affairs. It was re-ally a kind and gentle roast, consisting of many skits, each of which highlighted one of my idiosyncratic behaviors. It went long into the night, since my idiosyncrasies are legion.

In one skit, a group of six or so faculty members sat in a circle, mimicking an AA meeting, bemoaning the ways in which they had all succumbed to the scourge of "bifurcation," a particular nemesis of mine that I habitually brought up in conversation.

One particular troublesome bifurcation they dramatized was between the teaching and scholarly responsibilities for faculty at Christian colleges. This false choice was a failure to realize that effective teaching and good scholarship are two sides of the same coin, with each activity enriching the other.

Throughout this book, I will highlight some common false either/or choices Christians often face in conversations, reporting on how my involvement in inclusive conversations with believers from other Christian traditions has enabled me to move beyond truncated either/or positions that capture only partial truths to more comprehensive both/and positions.

#5: Failure to Build Bridges between the Christian Academy and the Christian Church

My first attempt to write a book in the early 1970s proved to be a dismal failure.

The context for this first major writing venture was my role in my local Lutheran church in Briarcliff Manor (New York) as a teacher in their adult discipleship program (Sunday school for adults). That early experience is an important part of my local church involvement to this day (which has expanded to my present responsibility for providing leadership for planning adult discipleship offerings for my current church home).

At that time, I was heavily involved in the personal task of seeking connections between what I was learning in the various academic disciplines and my biblical/theological understanding (the genesis of which I will report on in chapter 3). So, for a number of years, I taught a series of adult discipleship courses geared to the thinking layperson that gave a progress report on my attempts to make connections between two worlds of knowledge that most church members had bifurcated.

Toward the end of this series, the wild idea occurred to me that I should write a book reporting on the result of this personal quest for integration of knowledge that adults in many church settings could conceivably find helpful.

So I wrote a draft of a book titled *My Star: Reflections on Being a Person* (the title being inspired by the poem "My Star" by Robert Browning that ends with the words "What matter to me if their star is a world?/Mine has opened its soul to me; therefore I love it"[9]).

Since I was reporting on my search for connections between two commonly bifurcated worlds of knowledge, the 323 pages were about equally divided between my own personal narrative (designed to appeal to laypersons) and extended scholarly endnotes (designed to appeal to scholars in the Christian academy) detailing the connections I had uncovered between knowledge claims from the various academic disciplines and the biblical/theological understanding that was the focus of my personal narrative.

I sent this manuscript off to the editor of a major Christian publishing house. His eventual response was devastating. To paraphrase, "You can write a book that targets a 'popular' Christian church audience, or you can write a book that targets Christian

9. Browning, "My Star."

scholars working in the academy, but a book that targets both of these audiences is not possible." The unspoken assumption was that such a both/and book will not sell well.

This editor made a wise decision in light of the amateurish way in which I had bifurcated my book—using popular language in the body of my narrative and scholarly language in the extended endnotes. Not having the time to rewrite an integrated book, I decided to drop my dream of publishing it. The draft still sits on my bookshelves, gathering dust in two huge, blue, three-ring binders.

But this failed attempt to build bridges between the Christian academy and the Christian church did not deter me for long. Since I have been heavily involved for many years in both the Christian church and the Christian academy, I have continued working hard at such bridge-building. It is my hope that you will find this book to be a more successful attempt at such bridge-building in that it is written primarily in popular language geared to the thinking layperson, but it also integrates some scholarly language in places where I believe connections need to be made between biblical/ theological understanding and knowledge in the various academic disciplines.

What is the larger lesson I learned from the reasonable hesitancy of Christian publishing houses, from a financial standpoint, to publish books that attempt to address both members of the Christian academy and thinking laypersons within the church? Who will fill this vacuum?

The onus for that responsibility will lie primarily with the pastors and other leaders in Christian churches who share the conviction of Christian academics that it is important to seek connections between the academic disciplines and biblical/theological understanding. This important bridge-building role will include making sure that members of the Christian academy who attend a given church and members who are not scholars share their respective perspectives about whatever issue is being discussed.

In the concluding chapters of this book, I will make some more concrete recommendations for how to overcome this obstacle of a general failure to build adequate bridges between the Christian academy and the Christian church (as well as steps that can be taken to overcome the four other obstacles noted above).

Talking about Our Differing Partial Glimpses of the Truth

I believe that God knows the truth about all things. And, as one who aspires to be a follower of Jesus, I embrace with deep conviction his teaching that he came into the world to "testify to the truth" (John 18:37).

But the fact that I am not God presents a considerable challenge. My own quest for the truth and my aspiration to live out that truth are insatiable (sometimes I feel like my commitment to the Christian value of truth will consume me). But as a finite, fallible human being, I have only a partial glimpse of the truth that God fully understands. I "see in a mirror, dimly" (1 Cor 13:12).

I am not alone in my blurred vision of the truth. The same is true for another person whose partial glimpse of the truth may differ from mine. My partial glimpse is deeply informed by my personal story about my experiences during my pilgrimage, as well as by the various particularities of who I am, such as my gender, race/ethnicity, sexual orientation, and socioeconomic status. This leads me to see things in a particular way, which may differ from the perspective of a person who disagrees with me because her partial glimpse of the truth is informed by a different personal story and a different set of particularities.

So how do we seek truth together? We need to talk to each other about the substance of our differing partial glimpses of the truth, seeking first to understand the reasons for these differences in light of our differing personal biographies and particularities. She may see something that I have missed because of who she is, and I may see something she has missed because of who I am.

Having such dialogue about our disagreements does not succumb to sheer relativism, where one set of beliefs about a given issue is as good as another. Rather, the purpose of talking is to explore whether together we can arrive at a better approximation of the truth about the issue that is fully known only to God.

The distinguished Christian philosopher Nicholas Wolterstorff captures what I say above in more scholarly language when he notes that whereas the modern Enlightenment ideal was to seek after "generically human learning," where the scholar (and everyone else) must be stripped of all her particularities, the academy now generally accepts the view that much learning is perspectival, reflecting aspects of the scholar's social location, such as her personal story and her various particularities.[10]

In light of this diversity of belief about a given issue, Wolterstorff calls us to participate in "dialogic pluralism," which he describes as "a plurality of entitled positions engaged in dialogue which is aimed at arriving at truth."[11] The narrative that follows will exemplify such dialogic pluralism by attempting to give a fair representation of the agreements and disagreements among Christians about the nature of the truth they all seek.

An Overarching Theme: The Dynamism of Following Jesus

As teenagers at Fifty-Ninth Street Church, we used to flock to Saturday night church rallies, particularly attracted to announced sermon topics like "How to Find the Will of God for Your Life." An underlying assumption behind such sermons seemed to be that there was a static blueprint for each of our lives, and we needed all the help we could get to discern what that blueprint was as soon as possible, before we made irrevocable blunders.

I now believe that the idea of there being a blueprint for working out my aspiration to follow Jesus does not bear up under biblical scrutiny.[12] Rather, as I hope this book will amply demonstrate, there has been a dynamism in my attempt to follow Jesus.

10. Wolterstorff, "Scholarship Grounded in Religion." See also Heie, "Dialogic Discourse," 347–56.

11. Wolterstorff, "Scholarship Grounded in Religion," 14.

12. For example, Isaiah 58:10–11 reads, "If you offer your food to the

At any given time, I decide on a course of action that reflects my present understanding of what it means to follow Jesus. The results that emerge from this course of action help me to refine my understanding of what it means to follow Jesus. This refined understanding, in turn, informs my decision as to a subsequent course of action. This cycle then continues for the rest of my life.

In popular parlance, it is as I have "walked with Jesus" that I have gained greater insight into how to continue walking with Jesus.[13]

---

hungry and satisfy the needs of the afflicted, then . . . the Lord will guide you continually." This passage suggests that it is in the very process of helping others that you gain greater guidance as to how to continue helping others.

13. For an elaboration of the many nuances of this dynamism in my life, see Heie, *Learning to Listen*, 3–99.

CHAPTER 2

Feeling, Thinking, and Doing

Aspiring to Be a Whole Person

After I committed my life to Christ at the age of thirteen, I was discipled in a rather insulated, Pietist Lutheran church community. This left me with a view of personhood that was, for the most part, one-dimensional—my believing that the most important aspect of my commitment to the Christian faith was a deeply felt religious experience. But there was one very notable exception to that truncated view of personhood: my pastor.

Meet Pastor Omar

It is not unusual for me to wake up in the middle of the night with my mind racing about what transpired during the previous day or what's planned for the next day, especially when I am working on challenging writing projects. But this time it was the date itself that was on my mind.

It was about 4 a.m. on Thanksgiving morning (November 22, 2018) when I woke from a sound sleep, my mind racing with memories of former mentors—people who had a profound formative influence on my understanding of what it means to lead a faithful Christian life, people for whom I should be thankful, especially on Thanksgiving Day.

Pastor Omar Gjerness came immediately to mind. He assumed the position of senior pastor of Fifty-Ninth Street Church in Brooklyn around 1948, and I was in his first confirmation class as a thirteen-year-old. As I lay in bed thinking about Pastor Omar, it occurred to me that I had never thanked him. I decided that I needed to thank Omar as soon as possible.

Over breakfast that morning at the home of my brother-in-law Ken Peeders in Fergus Falls, Minnesota, I found out that Pastor Omar was in a nursing home in Fergus Falls. I decided to pay him a visit that morning, along with Ken and his brother Arnold, both whom had also been mentored by Omar at Fifty-Ninth Street Church.

Pastor Omar was in some pain as he lay in bed as a result of a fall. But even at age ninety-six, he was alert and in good spirits. He remembered, better than I did, a few of our interactions over the years (which included my worshipping from 1957 to 1959 at the church he served in Pasadena, California, while I was working at the Hughes Aircraft Company).

I quickly cut to the chase, thanking Pastor Omar for the enormous formative influence he had on me during our days together in Brooklyn and telling him how sorry I was that it had taken me seventy years to say thank you. I was delighted that I finally said thank you, and he seemed to be very appreciative. I am told that after that Thanksgiving morning meeting, Pastor Omar told a number of people how much our brief chat had meant to him.

Pastor Omar was one of the first people in my life who modeled the importance of holding to your beliefs with deep conviction, even passion. It was not unusual for his thoughtful sermons to be delivered with a degree of passion that brought him to unapologetic tears. More than anyone else, Pastor Omar taught me that it is important to feel deeply about your beliefs. But Pastor Omar was not into mindless emotionalism. His sermons were also filled with much food for thought. He beautifully exemplified that rare combination of a curious, probing intellect and an open, accepting heart.

Pastor Omar passed away on July 19, 2019. Although I procrastinated far too long, I am glad I finally took the initiative to thank him for his profound influence on my life. If you have not yet thanked someone who was a significant mentor for you, now may be a good time to send a note, email, or text expressing your gratitude.

Moving to a Comprehensive Perspective on Personhood as a Result of More Inclusive Conversations

The emphasis on feeling *and* thinking deeply about my beliefs that I learned from Pastor Omar is best understood in light of Fifty-Ninth Street Church being a congregation of the Pietist Lutheran denomination in America known as the Church of the Lutheran Brethren (CLB).

The various CLB congregations started in America were established by immigrants from Norway who, as products of the Pietist movement in Norway, had left the state Lutheran church in their homeland because of its perceived dead formalism and, upon arriving in America, wanted to create a Lutheran alternative with a Pietist emphasis. The main feature of this Pietist alternative was an emphasis on deeply felt religious experience, including feeling deeply about one's beliefs.[1]

Peter Gomes, the chaplain at Harvard University, captured the importance of feeling deeply with his reminder that we are not disembodied intellects—what he cleverly calls "minds on a stick."

But, despite Pastor Omar's splendid blending of feeling deeply and thinking deeply, many of my fellow worshippers at Fifty-Ninth Street Church had little use for the life of the mind. It isn't that they openly disparaged thinking deeply; it was more that serious intellectual pursuits were not as highly valued as deeply felt religious experiences.

1. My appreciation for some aspects of Pietism that were central to my upbringing in the Norwegian strain of Pietism was further strengthened when I worshiped during my days at Gordon College at the Community Covenant Church in West Peabody, Massachusetts, a congregation of the Evangelical Covenant Church of America, which has its roots in the Pietist movement in Sweden.

Having always loved studying and learning, it was like a breath of fresh air to eventually be exposed to Christians from the Reformed Christian tradition who highly valued the life of the mind. This exposure to theological otherness first came slowly among some faculty colleagues at both The King's College and Gordon College, and then, as more of a deluge, at Northwestern College in Iowa, which is affiliated with the Reformed Church of America. I arrived at Northwestern in 1980 to assume my first administrative position at a Christian college. The call to think deeply about one's Christian faith was front and center with my new Reformed friends.

But the Reformed tradition also had a downside, a temptation toward an arid intellectualism, a tendency on the part of some in that tradition to disparage the importance of deeply felt religious experiences. (I had the impression that a number of my new Reformed friends hadn't felt much of anything in years.)

My exposure to those embedded in the Reformed tradition also sowed the seeds for my realization of the importance of *doing* in following Jesus. But it was my immersion in a third Christian tradition that amplified for me the importance of this third dimension of personhood.

After eight years in the Reformed Christian tradition, I had the opportunity to immerse myself for six years in the Anabaptist/Mennonite Christian tradition at Messiah College in Pennsylvania. I learned to deeply appreciate the Anabaptist view that what you say you feel deeply and think deeply about is empty if you don't live it every day, with a particular emphasis on promoting peace.

My exposure to the Anabaptist tradition led me to reject an insidious view of the relationship between my will and the will of God—the mistaken view that God wishes to obliterate my will and replace it with God's will.

The Bible does not teach that God wishes to obliterate my will, which would make me into something like a stone.[2] Rather, God wishes to transform my will away from selfishhness, which is the essence of sin, into the likeness of Christ (2 Cor 3:18, 5:17). There should be a synergy of wills, God's and mine, as noted in

2. For elaboration, see Heie, *Learning to Listen,* 38–40.

Philippians 2:13: "For it is God who is at work in you, enabling you both to will and to work for His good pleasure." As I will propose in a later chapter, what God intends for my will is that I be so attuned to God's redemptive purposes for creation that I choose to exercise my will in harmony with God's will.

But there was also a downside in my experience with the Anabaptist tradition that evidenced itself in a very painful experience that you will read about eventually. It was a temptation to embrace a weak, negative view of peace as only the absence of conflict that led some of my Anabaptist friends to camouflage their disagreements, neglecting to speak up when they should have to address injustice, supposedly to keep the peace.

I am extremely thankful to God for the opportunity I had to be immersed in three differing Christian traditions. In a nutshell, the lessons I learned from my participation in more inclusive conversations with those embedded in these different traditions were these:

- All three Christian traditions taught me something important about how to be a follower of Jesus.

- None of these three traditions has captured all of God's truth about how to live well as a follower of Jesus.

- It was through listening well to deeply committed Christians in all three traditions that I was able to gain a more comprehensive view of what it means to be a faithful follower of Jesus.

- I need to embrace a comprehensive view of what it means to be a whole person following Jesus, which includes thinking deeply, feeling deeply, and living out my beliefs.

The comprehensive view of being a whole person that evolved for me is a synthesis of those aspects of personhood that psychologists name as the affective, the cognitive, and the volitional.

I am sure that if I had the opportunity to be immersed in a few other Christian traditions (e.g., the Wesleyan, Pentecostal, Roman Catholic, and Orthodox traditions), I would also learn some other lessons about how to live well as a whole person who aspires to follow Jesus.

The lessons I learned from my exposure to multiple Christian traditions lead me to offer a word of advice about the importance of exposing yourself to theological otherness:

Dare to step out of your comfort zone of listening only to those who share your Christian tradition. There is much to be learned by listening carefully to a diversity of deeply committed followers of Jesus whose Christians traditions can enlarge and enrich your understanding of what it means to faithfully follow Jesus.

If I had not had the opportunity to experience this diversity within Christian belief and practice, I would not have learned how to blend thinking, feeling, and doing. In the next chapter, I will report on how that blending informed my views about the goals of Christian higher education.

Excursus: An Example of My Own Blending of Thinking, Feeling, and Doing

I had just agreed to sell my 1972 Ford Grand Torino station wagon to a boyhood friend, Ken Jensen, who lived on Long Island. That car was a real calamity, getting about eight miles per gallon, downhill. After driving that huge blue monster for about a year, I couldn't afford to keep gas in it, and Ken, being mechanically inclined, unlike me, said he could work on improving the gas mileage. So I drove my car from my residence in Briarcliff Manor, New York, to Ken's home in Huntington Station. After completing our transaction, Ken graciously drove me to Grand Central Station in Manhattan, where I boarded a New York Central train headed for Briarcliff Manor late that afternoon.

As I sat quietly on the train, I felt a strong sense of relief at having been able to sell my car at the same time that I experienced a deep feeling of wonder at the sight of the spectacular sunset over the New Jersey Palisades.

Then I started thinking about one of the challenging institutional projects I was involved with at The King's College, a project on which I was making little progress. I was overwhelmed with an uncontrollable urge to pray about this project. It wasn't a matter of my praying because it was a time of day set aside for me to initiate prayer. Rather, praying seemed like the only natural (or supernatural?) thing to do. I could no sooner not pray than exit the moving train. In that moment, a radical thought occurred to me that revolutionized my thinking about prayer: in some mysterious way that I do not understand, God initiates my prayer. It is God who prompts me to pray, possibly through the situation in which I find myself, like marveling at the beauty of a sunset after feeling relief from unloading a disastrous car.

Since that experience on a fast-moving train, I have often wondered whether what transpired was a manifestation of what we Christians refer to as the "illumination of the Holy Spirit." We talked a lot about that during my Pietist upbringing, but I never had much clarity then as to what such talk might mean; nor do I now. Some might argue that God performed some type of cerebral miracle in my head, causing me to think something I wouldn't think otherwise. I see no need for such an explanation, although I cannot rule it out. As a natural scientist, I do believe in the possibility of miracles, since science can investigate only what typically happens under given antecedent conditions and must remain mute on the possibility or impossibility of miracles, which are atypicalities.

But I think that what happened on that train was much more ordinary. In some way that I cannot fully comprehend, the sight of a beautiful sunset reminded me of the work to which God had called me, and it was quite normal for me to commit that work to God once again. And if the work of the Holy Spirit includes bearing witness to God's redemptive intentions for all of creation made possible through Jesus Christ, then this situational prompting to commit to God my project at The King's College as I sat on that train qualifies as one possible manifestation of the illumination of the Holy Spirit.

Whether or not this experience is related to biblical teachings about the Holy Spirit, of one thing I am sure: I was feeling deeply *and* thinking deeply at the same time, and the results inspired me to roll up my sleeves the next day to continue working on my project. This illustrates well the truth about the necessity to live out what you say you believe and feel.

CHAPTER 3

The Integration of
Faith and Learning

Since all my formal higher education was under secular auspices, I had no idea what Christian higher education was all about. That would change as a result of the influence of another very significant mentor in my life. David Wolfe helped me to understand one possible aspect of the phrase "integration of faith and learning" that Christian institutions of higher education proclaimed as their most fundamental distinctive. But more inclusive conversations with some other Christian teachers and scholars led me to think about the possibility that my understanding of the integration of faith and learning was truncated and needed to be replaced by a more comprehensive view.

Meet David Wolfe

Very early on the morning of September 13, 1963, David Wolfe knocked on my door in the faculty apartment house in Ossining, New York (overlooking Sing Sing Prison) where we both lived at the beginning our teaching careers at The King's College. David had a phone and I didn't, so he passed along the message that I should drive quickly to St. Clare's Hospital in New Jersey where my wife was about to give birth to our first child. I immediately left for the hospital, thereby missing the first day of the fall faculty workshop

(I have met a number of college faculty since then who would have paid big bucks for an equally compelling excuse).

That was the beginning of a deep, lifelong friendship with a person who worshipped in the Baptist tradition.[1]

More than anyone else, David, a philosopher, has been my intellectual mentor. The context for his mentoring was that my formal education, all the way through my PhD, was totally devoid of struggling with any foundational philosophical/theological questions as I studied mechanical engineering and the aerospace sciences and learned how to teach mathematics. David initiated me into struggling with such foundational questions in two overlapping stages, primarily by recommending books and articles to read (I also audited the equivalent of a philosophy major under David's mentoring).

David first introduced me to questions about values (what philosophers call axiological questions). These questions interested me because of my intuitive sense that if you dig beneath the surface of any decision that you make, you will uncover one or more value commitments.

So, I considered in some depth the question "What value assumptions inform the work of mathematicians?"[2] It soon became obvious to me that questions about foundational value commitments can be asked of practitioners in any academic discipline.

Eventually, my search for foundational value commitments made by mathematicians led me to ask myself the broader question about the value commitments that were foundational for my Christian faith.

Therefore, during a sabbatical semester at The King's College, I carefully read through the entire Bible, word for word (even the book of Numbers), looking for biblical hints about what's important relative to God's purposes for creation. The results were mind-blowing.

1. After a distinguished teaching career at The King's College, Wheaton College, and Gordon College, David left teaching at a relatively young age, moving with his family to North Tunbridge, Vermont, where he served for many years as the pastor of a small community church.

2. My eventual response to that question can be found in Heie, "Mathematics: Freedom within Bounds."

The narrow view of God's redemptive purposes that was prominent in my Pietist Lutheran upbringing—that God is only concerned about salvation of individual persons—was shattered. I came to embrace a view that was prominent in the Reformed Christian tradition: that God wishes to redeem the entirety of the created order. All of God's creation groans for redemption (Rom 8:19–22). And God wishes to redeem all of it (Col 1:15–20; see also Acts 3:20–26, Eph 2:13–14, and 2 Cor 5:18–20).

Therefore, the call for Christians to "love your neighbor" (Matt 22:39) points to the Christian value of caring relationships between persons, which includes fostering the personal growth of others in accordance with their unique abilities and fostering peace and reconciliation between persons and groups in conflict. A special focus of caring for the well-being of others, as described in Matthew 25:31–46, is caring for the sick,[3] feeding the hungry, giving drink to the thirsty, providing clothing for the naked, welcoming the stranger, and visiting those in prison—all of which can be viewed as aspects of doing justice for the marginalized in society (called the "least of these" in verse 45).

But the call to redemptive work for those who claim to be followers of Jesus is even broader than caring for the well-being of others. It also includes being agents for a host of other redemptive efforts, including the flourishing of the natural creation, the uncovering of the truth about all aspects of God's creation, the repair of broken systemic structures in society (including the political realm), and the fostering of the Christian value of beauty found in God's creation and our human creativity.

Of course, no one follower of Jesus can do all of that. The teaching of 1 Corinthians 12 about the body of Christ is that each Christian can contribute to the realization of God's redemptive purposes in accordance with his or her particular gifts.

---

3. As I write these words, a host of doctors, nurses, and other medical practitioners are risking their lives to care for patients who have been victims of the coronavirus pandemic. Jesus, who cared deeply for the sick during his journey on earth, would certainly commend such heroic commitment to caring for the sick (see Matt 25:36).

The Integration of Faith and Learning

The second stage of David's mentoring revolved around broader consideration of the phrase "integration of faith and learning" that was, at that time, generally considered to be the most fundamental distinctive of Christian higher education. Let me set a context for these broader conversations.

As I was completing my graduate studies in the aerospace sciences at Princeton University, I decided that I wanted to enter college teaching rather than return to working in the aerospace industry. The primary source of my inspiration was my splendid experience as a teaching assistant for Princeton's Dr. Forman Acton, a professor of electrical engineering (another mentoring story that I will share in an addendum to this book).

But as I thought about institutions where I could possibly teach, I came to a realization that deeply informed my decision-making: I had become an entrenched intellectual dualist. I lived in two worlds of knowledge that never intersected: the world of my evolving biblical and theological understanding and the world of knowledge in the various academic disciplines I had studied.

Since it appeared to me that knowledge claims from various sources had to cohere, I had an intuitive sense that such intellectual dualism was unacceptable. The claim of Christian colleges was that they are committed to overcoming such dualism by seeking the integration of knowledge. So I decided to apply for a mathematics teaching position at The King's College, a Christian liberal arts college in Briarcliff Manor, New York, although I didn't have a clue at the time about how to even begin pursuing such integration.

Enter David Wolfe. During our first few years together, David helped me see that the quest for coherence of knowledge involved seeking connections between knowledge claims in the various academic disciplines and one's biblical and theological understanding.

Soon after David's mentoring ended (when he returned to his alma mater, Wheaton College in Illinois, to teach), I formulated a general strategy for seeking such connections in knowledge claims that focused on the posing of what I came to call "integrative questions." These are questions that by their very nature require one to draw deeply from knowledge in the academic disciplines and one's biblical and theological understanding.[4]

Here is a small sample of such integrative questions:

- Biology: To what extent should genetic engineering be used to enhance human well-being?

- Sociology/social work: To what extent are social problems caused by inadequacies in societal structures or by individual or group irresponsibility, or some of both?

- Fine arts: What are the limits, if any, on the freedom of human creative expression?

- Economics: What is the relationship between the quest for profitability and the Christian call for compassion and justice?

- Physics: What is the status of models in scientific inquiry, and what are the similarities and differences between the use of models in scientific inquiry and the use of models in theological inquiry?

- Psychology: Why do ordinary people sometimes do extraordinary evil (e.g., genocide and mass killings)?

Moving to a Comprehensive Perspective on the Integration of Faith and Learning Based on More Inclusive Conversations

My focus on posing integrative questions is very cerebral (cognitive), dealing with the world of ideas. In light of my argument in chapter 2 that Christians should wed (so to speak) thinking, feeling, and doing, isn't the cognitive focus on making connections between knowledge in the academic disciplines and biblical/theological

---

4. I eventually developed somewhat of a cottage industry promoting this Integrative Questions strategy in numerous national and regional faculty development workshops and retreats on behalf of the Council for Christian Colleges and Universities (CCCU). For some elaboration on this strategy, see Ostrander, *Why College Matters to God,* 118–22.

understanding[5] a truncated view of the meaning of integration of faith and learning? Yes!

I have been able to formulate a more comprehensive view about the nature of integrating faith and learning by engaging in more inclusive interactions (mostly through reading, rather than personal engagement) with three gifted Christian scholars: Doug and Rhonda Jacobsen, recently retired from serving at Messiah College,[6] and James K. A. Smith at Calvin College.

Formation or Information?

Smith asks some provocative questions about the nature of higher education, under Christian or other auspices, that call into question a truncated focus on the accumulation of information.

> What if education . . . is not primarily about the absorption of ideas and information, but about the *formation* of hearts and desires? . . . What if the primary work of education was primarily concerned with shaping our hopes and passions—our visions of "the good life"? . . . What if education wasn't first and foremost about what we know, but about what we love?[7]

Smith answers his own questions by proposing that his model for Christian education is "not primarily a matter of sorting out which Christian ideas to drop into eager and willing mind-receptacles; rather, it is a matter of thinking about how a Christian education shapes us, forms us, molds us to be a certain kind of people whose hearts and passions and desires are aimed at the kingdom of God."[8]

---

5. This cognitive focus on making connections between knowledge in the academic disciplines and one's biblical/theological understanding is often called the Reformed Calvinistic approach to the integration of faith and learning, and is often traced to the late distinguished Christian philosopher Arthur Holmes. See his *All Truth Is God's Truth* and *The Idea of a Christian College*.

6. Rhonda and "Jake" are good friends of mine; we served together at Messiah College from 1988 to 1993.

7. Smith, *Desiring the Kingdom,* 17–18 (emphasis original).

8. Smith, *Desiring the Kingdom*, 18.

The bulk of Smith's book is then devoted to the contours of his proposal that participation in Christian worship should be the primary vehicle for Christian colleges to foster such formation.

The Jacobsens strike a similar chord in their views about the nature of Christian scholarship:

> Christian scholarship becomes a matter of "living the questions" as much as it is a search for definitive answers.[9]

> Christian scholarship . . . would emphasize connections of one's scholarship to one's life as a whole.[10]

> The way we think and the way we live are intimately connected to one another. . . . Christian scholarship is ultimately a matter of living the questions; it is never a matter of thought alone.[11]

The Jacobsens then flesh out this comprehensive view by proposing a "threefold definition of scholarship that includes analytic, strategic, and empathic modes of reflection" that divide scholarship "along the lines of ideas, actions and feelings"—"analytic styles of scholarship are idea-oriented . . . strategic styles of scholarship are action-oriented . . . empathic styles of scholarship are feeling-oriented."[12]

Given my own belief that Christians should give expression to the cognitive, affective, and volitional dimensions of personhood, I embrace the broad contours of the proposals from Smith and the Jacobsens and thank them for helping me move beyond my original truncated view of the integration of faith and learning. But I do have a caveat.

9. Jacobsen and Jacobsen, *Scholarship and Christian Faith*, 45.

10. Jacobsen and Jacobsen, *Scholarship and Christian Faith*, 48.

11. Jacobsen and Jacobsen, *Scholarship and Christian Faith*, 60.

12. Jacobsen and Jacobsen, *Scholarship and Christian Faith*, 119, 124–25.

A Question for Further Consideration

Professor Smith's proposal about the primacy of formation over information does not fit well with my experience.

When I did my tour of the Bible, searching for hints about God's redemptive purposes for creation, I concluded that one of God's redemptive purposes is that Christians (and everyone else) gain greater understanding of the nature of all aspects of God's creation (which is what my posing of integrative questions is all about). In other words, my posing of integrative questions is not an intellectual exercise. Rather, it is a deep expression of love for God and my hopes for the full realization of the kingdom of God. It is not just a dispassionate collection of information. Rather, it has been integral to my formation as a Christian.

So my question for Professor Smith is whether his proposal may cause some readers to create an untenable bifurcation between formation and information that could be erroneously interpreted as diminishing the importance of thinking deeply. An indication that he does not intend such bifurcation is his proposal that Christian colleges provide more opportunities for "embodied learning" that "shapes character." For example, he proposes the possibility that "an advanced seminar in Continental philosophy" could "investigate a key theme in contemporary French thought—the shape of hospitality," and he proposes that "as a way of concretizing the issues in practice," the instructor could "require students in the seminar to adopt intentional practices of hospitality throughout the semester, working through the Service Learning Center."[13] It appears to me that such a course would create integral connections between information and formation.

I Want All of It, Not Just Some of It

I remember well the question posed by a visitor to The King's College many years ago during an event for prospective students: "I have been accepted to Dartmouth College. Why should I enroll at

---

13. Smith, *Desiring the Kingdom,* 228–29.

The King's College?" I didn't give a cogent response at the time, but I've since come up with the following: "If you want a top-notch education in the various nontheological academic disciplines, then go to Dartmouth. If you want a top-notch education in biblical/theological studies, then go to an excellent Bible institute (like Moody). But if you want an education that seeks to make connections between biblical/theological understanding and knowledge in the nontheological academic disciplines, then come to The King's College."

That response now seems quaint. Because it was this quest for integrated knowledge that propelled me into Christian higher education, I am saddened by recent conversations I have been privy to that barely mention the search for connections between biblical/theological understanding and knowledge in the academic disciplines as a fundamental distinctive of Christian higher education. It appears to me that a number of Christian colleges and universities have sacrificed this distinctive integrative quest for providing job training that can be obtained under many secular auspices, with the only claim to distinctiveness being that such training will be provided in a "safe environment" governed by numerous lifestyle rules. To the extent that this has happened, it violates what I have come to believe is the hallmark of Christian higher education at its best: *conversations seeking truth* (more about that at the very end of this book).

The insights from Professor Smith and the Jacobsens that this cognitive focus is truncated is correct. But that should not be used as an argument for its elimination or subordination to other foci. Rather, adequate attention must be given to a broad view of the integration of faith and learning that embraces three foci, as noted in the following advice to all those involved in Christian higher education:

As you seek to foster the ideal of integrating faith and learning, don't pick and choose between the cognitive, affective, and volitional aspects of such integration. Rather, seek for connections between these aspects of being a whole person.

My advice comports well with the reflection of the Jacobsens that "our point [in writing this book] is not to declare one model [for doing Christian scholarship] better than all others."[14] The "intention" of the Jacobsens is

> not to pronounce definitive answers [as to what Christian scholarship should look like] but to enlarge the conversation—to provide a framework that will better enable people who embody different styles of Christian scholarship to converse respectfully and intelligently with each other and with their other religious and non-religious peers in the academy.[15]

That desire for more inclusive conversations with those holding to different views is at the heart of this book.

Excursus: My Integrative Question
Blending Information and Formation

A student taught me the most important lesson I ever learned about teaching. I was sitting in my office in Harmony Hall at The King's College one morning, reading *Introduction to Psychology* by Atkinson and Atkinson. A student who would flunk out of college in about six weeks, despite being very bright, walked by my door and noticed what I was reading. He came into my office, dumbfounded because I was reading the assigned textbook for his Psych 101 course, a book that he had not yet opened. He asked me why I was reading this elementary book (after all, I had a BME, MSME, MA, and PhD), and I told him (as I will soon tell you). He then said something that revolutionized my view of teaching and learning: "The difference between you and me, Dr. Heie, is that you have a 'need to know,' and I don't." His perception, unfortunately, was that the content of this book had nothing to do with his life. My contrary deep conviction was that the content of this book had a great deal to do with my life. Throughout my teaching career after that experience, I have tried to create a "need to know" within my students, primarily by pointing out ways in which the questions we

---

14. Jacobsen and Jacobsen, *Scholarship and Christian Faith*, 29.
15. Jacobsen and Jacobsen, *Scholarship and Christian Faith*, xi.

were dealing with were not abstractions but were closely related to a desire to live well.

As I was beginning to struggle with the integrative question about the connection, if any, between my value commitments as a mathematician and my value commitments as a Christian, I also began wondering about another integrative question lingering from my Pietist upbringing: What is the relationship between law and liberty in a Christian ethic?

This question emerged as crucial for me because the ethical focus in my Pietist upbringing was defined largely in terms of proscriptions—a list of things Christians shouldn't do. This proscriptive ethical emphasis continued at The King's College: all of us (faculty and students) signed an annual pledge that we wouldn't participate in certain activities, like drinking alcoholic beverages and going to movies. In my early years at King's, this didn't bother me much. After all, it was consistent with my Pietist upbringing.

But I increasingly came to see the negative consequences of this ethical emphasis on a set of proscriptive rules. I still remember well the question posed by one of our students when she appeared before a student discipline committee because of a minor infraction of our rules: "When are you going to let us decide some things for ourselves, so we can grow up?" Increasingly, I came to the firm conviction that such a proscriptive legalistic approach to holiness had to go. But, what should I put in its place?

. An inviting alternative seemed to lie in the version of situation ethics being proposed by Joseph Fletcher[16] and others in the sixties. Just love! Just do what you judge to be the loving thing to do in the given situation. But as I read further about communities that claimed to live by this solitary maxim, I discovered that some very destructive behaviors were being perpetuated in the name of love. Some men considered women to be objects of sexual satisfaction because of a warped understanding of the meaning of love. So in my mind, this apparently open-ended approach to ethics also had to go. I found that I needed to formulate a more nuanced position between unacceptable extremes, which soon became the pattern in

---

16. Fletcher, *Situation Ethics.*

my intellectual pilgrimage as I sought to replace either/or positions with both/and positions. This started my lifelong quest to understand the proper relationship between law and liberty in a Christian ethic that I could live by.

As has already been hinted at, my present understanding of that relationship starts with embracing an expansive view of God's redemptive purposes (what I have called biblical values). In that light, I certainly need to avoid behaviors that are counter to God's redemptive purposes. But my positive ethical mandate is to plant tiny seeds of redemption that foster God's redemptive purposes (in ways that you will soon read about).

It should be obvious by now that my struggle with this primary integrative question has not been an intellectual exercise focused on gathering information. Rather, it has been central to my aspiration to live well as a follower of Jesus, thereby blending information and formation. And my need to blend information and formation emerged from my more inclusive conversations with other Christians about the most fundamental nature of Christian higher education.

CHAPTER 4

Political Domination, Withdrawal, or Conversation

Having embraced the belief that God intends for all of the created order to be redeemed, it was hard for me to imagine how that could be possible, even to a small degree, in the broken dysfunctional realm of American politics.

I had essentially been apolitical until about the age of forty. That changed when I met another significant mentor, Jim Skillen. But once my interest was piqued, I had a lot of catching up to do. I soon discovered two dominant views about how Christians in America should do, or not do, politics: domination or withdrawal. Dissatisfied with both of those strategies, I searched for a third way, which took me onto a path that I am still walking.

Meet Jim Skillen

After teaching mathematics for twelve years at The King's College, I made a parallel move to Gordon College in Wenham, Massachusetts, in the fall of 1975. That fall, I met Jim Skillen, who had just arrived at Gordon to teach political studies.

As already reported, it was the encouragement from David Wolfe while we were both teaching at The King's College that led me to struggle with the axiological question "What is important?" This, in turn, led to my exhaustive search through the Bible, looking for hints about the scope of God's redemptive purposes in terms of biblical values.

As I have also reported, my search through Scripture also led me to embrace a broad view of God's redemptive purposes, which included a calling for Christians to be agents for the redemption of broken systemic structures in society, including politics.

But was the idea of redeeming the broken political system in America only a pipe dream in the fall of 1975 (as it certainly appears to be again now as I write these words)?

Enter Jim Skillen. Prior to having conversations with Jim, my theoretical musings about God's desire to redeem the political system in America were just a lot of talk, with no actions to back them up. In 1975, I was essentially apolitical, not having given much thought to the possible role that Christians could and should play in American politics.

My conversations with Jim changed all of that. At the time, Jim was shaping a fledgling organization that started in 1977 (the Association for Public Justice), which would eventually become the Center for Public Justice (CPJ). Jim served as the founding director and then president until his retirement in 2009. Over the many years of our deep friendship,[1] I have been inspired by Jim's consistent engagement in respectful conversation with those who have disagreed with him, an example that has greatly encouraged me in my own efforts to orchestrate respectful conversations.

One particular focus of CPJ (a call for "confessional pluralism") was an important factor in my evolving thinking about how I believe Christians should do politics.

---

1. I served with Jim for a number of years as a member of the CPJ board of trustees.

Evolution toward a Conversational Approach to Doing Politics that Dismantles a Few Bifurcations along the Way

As my thinking about how Christians should do politics evolved, a few themes emerged that I will now present in no particular order, noting some common bifurcations that fell along the wayside.

Christians Should Go Public with Their Claims to Knowledge

Many in our culture believe that it is acceptable for Christians to express their beliefs in private (among family and friends and in their Christian communities). But beliefs based on Christian commitments, or any other religious commitments, should not be expressed in public political discourse.

I now reject that bifurcation between private and public expressions of beliefs based on religious commitments and embrace the principle of confessional pluralism that CPJ espouses. This principle holds that government must protect with equal treatment under the law the variety of religious and secular communities within its jurisdiction without giving preferential treatment to any one community. Therefore, in the political realm, everyone should have the opportunity to publicly express their beliefs about any political issue being considered, even those beliefs based on religious commitments.

My motivation to reject the private/public bifurcation relative to political discourse and to embrace of the CPJ principle of confessional pluralism is based on two reasons. The first is my calling into question the common view that the problem with religious people bringing their beliefs into the public square is that their beliefs are based on certain value commitments while those holding to secular beliefs are value-neutral. That is blatant nonsense. No one is value-neutral.[2] Everyone has a set of value commitments that inform her or his beliefs about political issues. Therefore, there should be an

2. Clouser, *Myth of Religious Neutrality.*

even playing field in public political discourse, with everyone having an equal voice.

My second reason for rejecting the private/public bifurcation relative to political discourse harkens back to my acceptance of a position Nicholas Wolterstorff has taken. Wolterstorff argues there is no such thing as "generically human learning."[3] All claims to knowledge are informed by our particularities, which include our personal pilgrimages that have led us to embrace certain worldview beliefs, be they religious or secular. Again, this calls for an even playing field for all of us relative to political discourse. The way Wolterstorff puts it relative to academic communities—which I believe can be extended to all communities, including communities involved in doing politics—is that we all need to embrace a "dialogic pluralism" that is characterized by a "plurality of entitled positions engaged in dialogue which is aimed at arriving at truth."[4]

Separation of Church and State Properly Understood

One of the most significant accomplishments of America's Founding Fathers is that they had the wisdom to erect a high wall of separation between church and state. As stated in the First Amendment to the Constitution, "Congress shall make no law respecting an establishment of religion or prohibiting the free exercise thereof."

I believe this wise stipulation was intended to be applied at the institutional level. No church body—such as a particular church, synagogue, or mosque; or a particular grouping of churches, synagogues or mosques, such as a Christian church denomination representing a particular Christian tradition (e.g., Baptists, Presbyterians)—should be given preferential treatment. And no church body should be prevented from practicing their particular religious commitments, provided that these practices fall within other laws of the land.

But it is an error to interpret this wise stipulation as prohibiting individual religious or secular persons from bringing their

3. Wolterstorff, "Scholarship Grounded in Religion," 13.
4. Wolterstorff, "Scholarship Grounded in Religion," 14.

religious or secular worldview commitments to public political discourse. As argued above, all Americans should have the opportunity to bring their worldview beliefs to public political discourse on an even playing field.

Domination Is Not an Option

Some Christians argue that the results of political legislation should exclusively reflect Christian beliefs. This call to dominate legislative outcomes is often based on a belief that America was founded as a Christian nation. This belief does not stand up to close scrutiny.[5]

Although many of America's Founding Fathers were Christian Deists, they wisely avoided establishing Christianity or any other religion as a national religion, the precepts of which would have to be practiced by all Americans. They believed that the laws of the land must be legislated by a democratic process where proponents of diverse worldview beliefs, religious or secular, have an equal voice.

Of course, we Christians hope that the laws of the land will reflect Christian values, since these values are, in our estimation, human values. But adherents to other worldviews, religious or secular, believe the same to be true of their particular value commitments. Government should not give a priori preference to any set of value commitments during political deliberations.

Two-Kingdom Lutheranism Is Not an Option

I don't recall Pastor Omar ever explicitly preaching a sermon about two-kingdom theology during my early discipleship as a Christian at the Pietist Lutheran Fifty-Ninth Street Church. But I later discovered this particular focus of Lutheranism and came to reject it.

In brief, my understanding of the Lutheran teaching about two kingdoms is based on making a distinction between law and gospel that works like this: when I am functioning as a citizen of my country—serving in public office, for example—I abide by the laws of the land (as should everyone else) regardless of whether those

5. Fea, *Was America Founded?*

laws reflect the teachings of the gospel of Jesus that I embrace. But I live out my gospel beliefs in a nonpublic realm, such as my home and church.

While holding to the separation of church and state at the institutional level, the problem I have with this two-kingdom perspective at the personal level is that it creates an untenable bifurcation relative to who I am as a person. While granting that there may be some different rules of the game when I function in two different realms of responsibility,[6] I am not two different persons. I hold to certain foundational value commitments to which I must be true in all of my life, not one set of value commitments when operating in the public realm and a different set when operating in the private realm. The conversational model for political involvement that I will soon be recommending for all Christians will reflect this coherence.

Withdrawal Is Not an Option

Having rejected the domination model for Christian involvement in politics, an alternative is to just withdraw from political involvement. I also reject this approach because I believe that God wishes to redeem all aspects of life, including the political realm, and Christians are called to be agents for God's redemptive purposes, with each Christian contributing in accordance with his or her giftedness.

But my conversations with Christian friends in the Anabaptist/Mennonite tradition have revealed a spectrum of views regarding whether Christians should do politics. Some in that tradition believe that politics is so broken by human sinfulness that Christians should withdraw from political involvement, choosing rather to model a Christian way to live well together in their church

---

6. This assertion comports with the principle of "structural pluralism" embraced by the Center for Public Justice (CPJ), which holds that it is government's obligation to recognize and do justice to the variety of nongovernmental responsibilities that belong to humans by virtue of their created identities. This requires constitutional limits of governmental jurisdiction so that government does not subsume nongovernmental institutions and associations under its direct authority.

communities. Others encourage active political involvement on the part of Christians, not in place of, but in addition to such modeling in Christian communities.

Given my antipathy toward bifurcations, I embrace a both/and, rather than an either/or, position. In what follows, I will share my understanding of how the late John Howard Yoder, the most distinguished of recent Anabaptist theologians, appears to accept this both/and position, drawing primarily on his classic book *The Politics of Jesus*.

A Radical Political Option Modeled by Jesus

It is first important to note Yoder's assertion that "it is a fundamental error to conceive of the position of the church in the New Testament as a 'withdrawal.'"[7] That Yoder is not proposing Christians should withdraw from modern society or government is further emphasized elsewhere in his writings. For example:

> I am not advocating systematic abstention from modern society, or even from "government," as the "Christ against culture" caricature of H. Richard Niebuhr . . . would have it.[8] . . . I am rather pointing to a great variety of styles of involvement, of which "the sword" should not be the dominant paradigm.[9]

Relative to involvement with government (political action), Yoder goes on to propose that Christians exercise a "radical political option" modeled by Jesus.

> This study makes the claim that Jesus is, according to the biblical witness, a model of radical political action.[10]

7. Yoder, *Politics of Jesus*, 151.
8. Niebuhr, *Christ and Culture*.
9. Yoder, *Priestly Kingdom*, 164–65.
10. Yoder, *Politics of Jesus*, 12.

> The ministry and claims of Jesus are best understood as presenting to men not the avoidance of political options, but one particular social-political-ethical option.[11]

But what is the substance of the "radical political option" for Christians that Yoder is proposing? In addition to his position that the sword will not be the dominant paradigm, here are some other partial glimpses into some aspects of Yoder's thinking about an alternative paradigm for Christians doing politics.

- *Servanthood* replaces domination.[12]

- *Nonviolence* replaces the use of the sword,[13] except for certain judicial and police functions.[14]

- Although the radical political option modeled by Jesus may lead to a *cross*,[15] it will be "effective" (the "model of *Christian social efficacy*"[16] that will "determine the meaning of history"[17] is the Christian "political alternative to both insurrection [a quest for domination] and quietism [withdrawal]"[18]).

---

11. Yoder, *Politics of Jesus,* 234.

12. Yoder, *Politics of Jesus,* 134.

13. Yoder, *Politics of Jesus,* 250.

14. Yoder, *Politics of Jesus,* 205. My way of expressing this view of a limited use of the sword, consistent with the teachings of Romans 13:1–7, is that the radical political option to which Yoder calls Christians does not preclude reasonable coercive methods (e.g., requiring obedience to the laws of the land) to maintain law and order and appropriate punishment for those who violate the law. My own view as to appropriate punishment for violating the law is deeply informed by the restorative justice movement, which has a strong focus on rehabilitation of the offender in the context of attempts to restore positive relationships between the offender and the victim, as well as healing the harm done within the communities in which the offender and the victim are embedded. Much of the pioneering work for the restorative justice movement was done by the Mennonite scholar Howard Zehr. See Zehr, *Changing Lenses.* In the interest of full disclosure, I note that my daughter-in-law, Tammy Krause Heie, served as a teaching assistant for Professor Zehr at Eastern Mennonite University.

15. Yoder, *Politics of Jesus,* 45.

16. Yoder, *Politics of Jesus,* 250 (emphasis original).

17. Yoder, *Politics of Jesus,* 238.

18. Yoder, *Politics of Jesus,* 43.

- Exemplifying this radical political option will call for *patience*.[19]

On Being Reformed and Anabaptist

Although I have learned something important about how to follow Jesus from all the Christian traditions in which I have been immersed and I do not like to put anyone in a theological box (including myself, since I am rather eclectic theologically), I now feel most comfortable embracing a hybrid of being Reformed and Anabaptist.

I embrace the Reformed view that God wishes to reform all of the created order, including the political realm. But I also embrace a belief that the means of partnering with God in God's redemptive work should comport with the Anabaptist commitment to nonviolence and servanthood. In my own words, I should be a peacemaker in my attempts to foster God's redemptive purposes (in a way that I will soon explain). Holding both of these commitments in tension has been, and continues to be, a challenge.

My Conversational Model for Political Involvement

As the title for this chapter indicates, I describe three options for Christian participation in the political realm: withdrawal, domination, and conversation. Up to this point, I have rejected the withdrawal and domination models.

The model I now embrace is that of conversation, which is my exemplification of the radical political option proposed by John Howard Yoder. I saw this conversational model beautifully demonstrated in an online debate on my website, the highlights of which I presented in my recent book, *Reforming American Politics: A Christian Perspective on Moving Past Conflict to Conversation*. In chapter 11 of my book[20] I propose these steps as a way forward for Christians who desire to be agents for reforming American politics.

19. Yoder, *Politics of Jesus,* 238.
20. Heie, *Reforming American Politics,* 365–407.

The steps exemplify Yoder's radical political option and are based on commitment to a number of Christian values, including love, humility, courage, respect, truth, shalom, justice, patience, and hope. They can also be viewed as an attempt at peacemaking.

- *Develop personal relationships of mutual understanding and trust with those with whom you have political disagreements.*

- *Listen carefully to those who disagree with you about political issues (as a deep expression of love) and, when you adequately understand their reasons for their positions, engage them in respectful conversation about your agreements and disagreements toward the goal of finding some common ground and illuminating remaining disagreements.*

- *Reach across the political aisle or dining room table to seek both/ and positions that reflect the best insights of those on both sides of the aisle or table.*

A key element in my conversational model for doing politics addresses an enormous problem in American politics today: political inequality. Although denying or suppressing the right to vote for any citizen is an egregious sign of political inequality, the problem is deeper than that.

As political scientist Kim Conger has pointed out,[21] the deeper problem is that not everyone has an "equal stake" in the political system; majority voices too often overrule minority voices. Particularly problematic is the way in which "campaign donations buy access and attention," which too easily results in silencing the average voter and, especially, the marginalized members of our society. Therefore, what is needed is an even playing field in which every American citizen, independent of his or her resources or status in society, is able to participate equally in the political process by first being given a voice. As you will eventually see, from my Christian perspective, the need for such a deep level of political equality is based on a premise that is fundamental to this entire book: Jesus calls his followers to love others, and you don't love someone whom you have silenced.

21. Heie, *Reforming American Politics,* 192–99.

The apparent Achilles heel in these aspects of a conversational model for doing politics is that they run counter to the hyper-partisanship that prevails in our broken political realm. However, I can point to two examples where implementation of such a conversational model has yielded common ground.

My first example is presented in depth in my *Reforming American Politics* book, which reports on an online immigration reform conversation that I hosted on my website, respectfulconversation. net, between Robert McFarland, a professor of law at Faulkner University in Montgomery, Alabama, and Matthew Soerens, the US director of church mobilization at World Relief.[22]

As Christians, both Robert and Matthew appealed to the concept of justice, albeit focusing on two different dimensions of that contested concept. Robert focused on the retributive dimension of justice, arguing that those immigrants who have entered the country illegally should be held accountable. Matthew focused on the distributive dimension of justice, arguing that the quest to help everyone flourish implies that undocumented immigrants ought to be provided a pathway to citizenship.

At first, there appeared to be an impasse. But Matthew overcame that apparent impasse by proposing a both/and solution that provides a pathway to citizenship while also penalizing those who have entered the country illegally by means of appropriate fines instead of the draconian punishment of deportation that is tearing apart many Latino families.

Robert found Matthew's proposal to be "reasonable," adding that this is a "better proposal than outright amnesty." (Matthew's proposal does not call for amnesty, since it includes penalties in the form of fines.) This progress toward an acceptable both/and position occurred because Robert and Matthew were willing to respectfully listen to and talk to each other about their agreements and disagreements regarding immigration.

My second example of a conversational model leading to the uncovering of common ground occurred in the halls of the US Congress in 2013, when a bipartisan "gang of eight" senators

22. Heie, *Reforming American Politics*, 210–47.

collaborated to forge a comprehensive immigration reform bill. The Border Security, Economic Opportunity, and Immigration Modernization Act of 2013 reflected the best thinking of representatives of both major parties. It included both improved border security and an arduous pathway to citizenship that included the imposition of fines for having entered the country illegally (like Matthew's proposal). The Senate passed this bill by a vote of 68 to 32.

Alas, this comprehensive immigration reform bill was not considered by the House of Representatives. While the reasons were complex and multifaceted, I can't help but wonder whether the House would also have approved this bill, or a variation thereof, if they too had embraced a conversational model for doing politics by forming a bipartisan group of representatives willing to talk and listen to each other.

CHAPTER 5

Listening Well as
a Foundation for Leadership

I left teaching when I was my best at it. After seventeen years doing what I loved to do in the classroom, I took the administrative plunge. How can I explain such apparent craziness?

As a faculty member at both Gordon College and The King's College, I had carried out a number of quasi-administrative responsibilities, such as chairing key faculty committees, providing leadership for major curricular reform, and authoring two accreditation self-study reports. But to do administrative work full-time had the potential to exemplify the Peter Principle: being promoted to my level of incompetency.

When word got out that I was considering an appointment as vice president of academic affairs at Northwestern College in Orange City, Iowa, a faculty colleague at Gordon College who was and remains a dear friend asked to meet with me. Among other things, he wondered out loud whether I was "tough enough" for a VPAA position. Would I be able to criticize faculty who were not measuring up to performance standards?

Despite this expression of concern and my uncertainty about whether I would do well as an academic administrator, I accepted this VPAA position in the fall of 1980 for reasons I will soon share. But first you need to meet another one of my mentors, someone whose writing about the nature of leadership captures so beautifully the view of leadership that I learned to embrace during my on-the-job training as an academic administrator. It's a view that focused on the importance of a collaborative leadership style that started with listening well as the most important element of effective leadership in any organization.

Meet Parker Palmer

All my mentors you have met up to this point have been close personal friends who have influenced me through face-to-face engagements, including many conversations.

I have also had numerous mentors from a distance—writers and thinkers (whose books and articles were often recommended by my face-to-face mentors) who have had a profound influence on my evolving understanding of what it means to be a faithful follower of Jesus.

One such long-distance mentor has been Parker Palmer, a renowned sociologist who worships in the Quaker tradition. I have heard him speak twice, but we have never had a face-to-face conversation.

Nevertheless, I have been mentored in a powerful way by my reading of a number of his books, most notably *The Courage to Teach, To Know as We Are Known, Healing the Heart of Democracy,* and *The Active Life.*

The following passage from *The Active Life* informs the overall message of this book in a profound way by pointing to the only approach to leadership that fosters community between persons.

> Jesus exercises the only kind of leadership that can evoke authentic community—a leadership that risks failure (and even crucifixion) by making space for other people to act. When a leader takes up all the space and preempts all the action, he or she may make something happen, but the something is not community. Nor is it abundance, because the leader is only one person, and one person's resources invariably run out. But when a leader is willing to trust the abundance that people have and can generate together, willing to take the risk of inviting

people to share from that abundance, then and only then may true community emerge.[1]

The Emergence of a Collaborative Leadership Style

So why did I leave teaching, which I really loved and excelled at, for an administrative position? I welcomed the pay raise; no more teaching as an adjunct faculty member at two other colleges while teaching full-time at Gordon College just to keep food on the table. But, as you should have surmised by now, my career choices have never been informed primarily by salary considerations.

It was a vision that prompted this career move—a vision that I could see only through the eyes of faith. As a math teacher, I had, as a result of David Wolfe's mentoring, worked hard at making connections between my understanding of the nature of mathematics and my evolving biblical and theological understanding. I did so by focusing primarily on the values that underlie mathematical activity and the fit, or not, of those values with the values to which I was committed as a Christian.

The wild idea then occurred to me that it would be marvelous if I could inspire an entire college faculty to become as involved as I had been in seeking to make connections between their respective academic disciplines and their biblical and theological understandings. This is my Exhibit A in support of my view of Christian living as a dynamic process, where in the midst of seeking to live faithful to your understanding of what it means to follow Jesus, you subsequently gain greater insight in to how to continue following Jesus.

My first week as VPAA at Northwestern College was miserable. I was literally in tears as I drove to work one morning. I didn't know where to start. So for about a week I just read the material in the many folders that my predecessor had left me (uff da!). But then a thought occurred to me that set the stage for the rest of my tenure at Northwestern and the rest of my life. I will have a face-to-face conversation with each of my faculty members, being careful first to listen well.

1. Palmer, *Active Life*, 138.

So I arranged to have a conversation with each faculty member, about fifty to sixty in number, as I recall, in their offices. I asked each of them to be prepared to respond to the following two questions: "What is your vision for your own growth as a teacher and scholar into the near future?" and "What is your vision for the future of Northwestern College?"

These conversations were delightful and led to two marvelous results. First, I gained valuable insights into how I could begin shaping the future of Northwestern College to fit both my vision and the dreams of my faculty. Secondly, and even more importantly, I began developing relationships of mutual understanding and trust that would enable me to collaborate with faculty members toward making our respective visions come true.

That was the first step in the emergence of my collaborative leadership style—a step built on the primacy of building thriving personal relationships by first listening well. But how did that eventually translate into the nitty-gritty of carrying out my leadership responsibilities? A hint is provided by another skit during my belated going-away party at Messiah College where six Messiah College professors sat in a rowboat and began rowing (without the benefit of any water). They were poking fun at a primary strategy of my collaborative leadership style dubbed "Harold getting his oar in the water." Here is an example of how that worked.

Like most colleges, faculty governance at Messiah made professors responsible for formulating academic policies and designing the curriculum.

For example, the faculty at Messiah had responsibility for formulating and implementing the criteria for faculty promotion in rank and the granting of tenure. I believed that the present criteria needed significant improvement. I needed to share that conviction with the Faculty Rank and Status Committee while honoring their responsibility to formulate changes. I did both things by "getting my oar in the water."

My letter to the committee chair asking the committee to review the current criteria for promotion and tenure and develop recommendations for refinement also included a first draft of my ideas for improvement in light of my vision for the college as well as the visions of professors I had talked to. But I held my first draft lightly by saying, in effect, the following: "Here is my initial thinking about how to improve the present criteria for promotion and tenure. But that assignment is now in your capable hands. I will be very disappointed if you do not improve on my initial thinking."

This "getting my oar in the water" strategy flows from my understanding of the first portion of the advice on effective leadership given by Parker Palmer. Presenting Palmer's advice in my own words, he's saying that when the leader exercises a command-and-control style of leadership, the result will be only as good as that leader's giftedness. But when the leader dares to collaborate with followers, there is potential for the result to reflect the combined giftedness of the leader and followers.

But the second portion of Palmer's exhortation is equally compelling. When the leader effectively collaborates with followers, it builds a strong sense of community—a sense of interdependence, where we are all in this together.

Putting this insight into practice was an answer to my colleague who had asked whether I would be tough enough to be an effective VPAA. I discovered that as a result of my collaborative leadership style that focused on listening well, I was able to build strong personal relationships of mutual understanding and trust. These relationships enabled me to have honest, respectful, and productive conversations with individual faculty members at the end of performance reviews.

The way that worked was that at the end of each performance review (carried out jointly by the Faculty Status Committee and me), I wrote a detailed letter to the faculty member in which I first expressed my deep gratitude for his/her strengths as a faculty member. With that as the foundation, I then pointed out areas where the performance evaluation revealed that improvement (further personal growth) was needed.

This detailed letter was the starting point for a fruitful face-to-face conversation. One of my fondest memories of one such conversation was when a faculty member who was not promoted concluded our meeting by thanking me for my honesty, saying that

I was the first boss who had the courage to tell him where he needed to improve.

I believe that the reason this approach to faculty evaluation generally (not always) worked so well is that the faculty member and I had developed a personal relationship of mutual understanding and trust that enabled him or her to see that I was not suggesting a need for improvement from a supposed perch of superiority or authority. Rather, I was primarily interested in helping him or her to grow toward his or her maximum potential as a faculty member and as a person beloved by God, and therefore loved by me as well.

The above reflections comport well with an important distinction that Arthur Brooks has made,[2] drawing on the work of Daniel Goleman,[3] between authoritative leadership and authoritarian leadership.

> Authoritative leaders, according to Goleman, are visionaries who set a course for an institution and inspire each member to take responsibility for getting to the final destination.
>
> While authoritative leaders promote their own overarching vision, they are not *authoritarian.* They do not suppress dissent, instead granting employees the freedom to disagree and solve problems on their own.[4]

The primary lesson I have learned about myself over many years of trying to model authoritative, collaborative leadership is that what I do best is helping others do their best. All of the above can be summarized in the following advice for those who are in leadership positions anywhere:

Help those you lead do their best by first listening to their dreams for themselves and your organization and then providing them with a safe and welcoming space to work together with you to accomplish your shared vision.

---

2. Brooks, *Love Your Enemies,* ch. 3, "Love Lessons for Leaders," 65–85.
3. Goleman, "Leadership That Gets Results."
4. Brooks, *Love Your Enemies,* 78 (emphasis original).

When the Roof Fell in

Alas, my commitment to a collaborative leadership style has not always been shared by those to whom I reported. In fact, it led to me being fired as VPAA at Messiah College. It is important to briefly describe this painful part of my story because it has contributed significantly to my proposal in the last chapter of this book for creating more inclusive conversations among followers of Jesus.

It was the morning of August 3, 1993. When I arrived in my office that morning, my splendid administrative assistant, Shirley Groff (who did a lot of the work for which I received most of the credit), told me that President Hostetter wanted to see me in his office as soon as possible. I didn't know why. But I suspected it was to commend me for the results of an evaluation of my performance as VPAA that my faculty had recently completed. (Although I had not seen the results, rumor had it that these results were very laudatory.)

My hope for a commendation was shattered when, as I walked into President Hostetter's office, I saw that the chair of the board of trustees and another member of the executive committee of the board were already seated. That was not a good sign.

President Hostetter got right to the point. My tenure as VPAA was to be immediately terminated due to my "lack of deference to the president and board of trustees." I believe that what was interpreted as a "lack of deference" was that my collaborative leadership style conflicted with the command-and-control authoritarian leadership styles of both President Hostetter and the board of trustees.[5]

But it was the aftermath of my firing that had the greatest impact on shaping my proposal for more inclusive conversations among followers of Jesus.

It is an understatement to say that my faculty were not happy with my termination. To calm the troubled waters, the president and board hired the mediating services of a renowned peacemaker from the Anabaptist Christian tradition who had a splendid reputation for successful conflict resolution.

The details of this mediation process were never shared with me. I am told that there was a rather tumultuous meeting involving

---

5. For more details, see Heie, *Learning to Listen,* 68–75.

the faculty, President Hostetter, and the mediator. And I am guessing that the mediator spoke privately with the president and at least some of the trustees. But what shocked me and added significantly to the pain I experienced was that this mediator never spoke to me. How could that be, since it was my firing that led to the conflict? Shouldn't the mediator be interested in hearing my side of the story?

My pain from having been silenced was significantly alleviated a month or two after my firing when a board member showed up unannounced at the door of my home. I didn't know him well and he wasn't on the executive committee of the board (which I had been led to believe made the final decision to terminate my employment). After I welcomed him into my home, he simply said: "Harold, I want to hear your side of the story."

These few words were a marvelous gift. Finally, a person in authority with a commitment to listening invited me to share my pain. I cannot find words to adequately express the joy this kind gesture brought to me. Although it did not change the outcome, a sense of peace washed over me—like coming across an oasis during a desert journey.

Finally, someone wanted to listen to me. As he left my home that sunny morning, I felt not only listened to, but also loved.

That splendid gift has been the single greatest influence on how I have attempted be an agent for God's redemptive purposes for the twenty-eight years that have followed. Stated most succinctly: *You don't love someone whom you have silenced.* Stated positively (in more than twelve words): *To give someone who disagrees with you a safe and welcoming space to express that disagreement and then to talk respectfully about your disagreement is a deep expression of love.*

Excursus: Meet Mom and Pop

In a radio interview with a newspaper reporter shortly after the release of my *Reforming American Politics* book, I was asked to share the source of my strong commitment to listening well as a first step toward engaging in respectful conversations about disagreements. The seeds for this passion were sown around the dining room table during my boyhood days in Brooklyn; the planting was done by two of my most influential mentors, my mom and my pop (Nelly and Henning). I will explain this by repeating a slightly edited portion of the memoir I published in 2007, *Learning to Listen, Ready to Talk: A Pilgrimage toward Peacemaking*.[6]

Our home in Brooklyn was a welcoming space for the "girls." That is what Mom called her unmarried lady friends, who, like Mom, had emigrated from Norway in the 1920s and taken positions as maids and cooks in fine homes in New York City and Long Island.

Aagot, Elisabeth, Sophie, Johanna, and others flocked to our home on weekends for good food and good conversation, staples in the lives of Norwegians in Brooklyn. They were a lively group, some having strong opinions on most everything, including whether the pot roast was done well enough. I sensed they didn't have much opportunity to give voice to their points of view during the working week, possibly due to their perceived subordinate stations in life and their occasional struggles with the English language. Mom's facility with English had come a long way since her first job as a maid shortly after arriving in the States. One day when the lady of the house fell down the stairs, Mom blurted out one of the few English phrases she had learned, "Good for you." For emphasis, Mom said it a second time.

In our home, these women were given a safe and welcoming space to say whatever was on their minds, sometimes half in Norwegian and half in English. And even at those times when Mom's views, possibly on the pot roast, were the subject of criticism, Mom smiled, listened patiently, and gave a gentle response. Pop mostly listened, as did my twin brother John and I.

Mom, Pop, and the girls are no longer with us. But, in ways I have come to realize only fully recently, these good experiences of a safe and welcoming space for all of us around the table had a profound formative influence on me. I never thought much about it at the time because it was just the way things were in our home, like the air we breathed.

6. Heie, *Learning to Listen*, 3–4.

However, there was also a painful flip side to my experiences at home when the girls were not visiting us. While Mom created a welcoming space for the girls, she didn't always create such space for Pop. Part of the reason may be that while Mom loved to talk, Pop was the quietest person I have ever known. In later years, when John and I were out of the house, we used to compare notes on our telephone conversations with Pop. His typical response to our comments was "yup." Sometimes we had a five-yup conversation. When Pop was particularly effusive, the yups would go into double digits.

Besides personality differences, a deeper reason for Mom's lack of openness to Pop's points of view had to do with their differences about religion. In Norway, Mom had made a strong commitment to the Christian faith under the influence of the Pietist Lutheran Free Church. Pop was raised in the state Lutheran church in Norway but made no personal commitment to the Christian faith. I can't remember Mom and Pop ever talking, in the presence of their twin sons, about their differing views on the Christian faith. Although Pop was very quiet, I think, in retrospect, that he would have been willing to talk with Mom about their religious differences if he had sensed that Mom would provide a safe and welcoming space for him to express his particular point of view. Mom's views were set in cement. She didn't provide Pop with space to disagree. And I wasn't mature enough to know how to help Mom do that.

There were times when I wished Mom would stay home from church to be with Pop, to just listen and talk. I sensed that Pop thought there was significant contradiction between Mom's profession of Christian faith and her lack of openness to his point of view. In an unusual twist of providence, Pop did eventually make his own commitment to the Christian faith, in his seventies, after Mom had passed away. I believe Pop experienced the freedom and empowerment to make that choice only after Mom was gone.

Both the joyful results of our home being a welcoming space for the girls and the painful results of it not always being a welcoming space for Pop were the earliest seeds for a deep conviction that has matured since my boyhood days: *in my engagement with another person, I should first be a good listener, creating a safe and welcoming space for that person to have a voice.* They need hospitable room to express their points of view, even if I disagree. It is only within such a welcoming place that there is any hope for respectful conversation about our differences that will enable us to learn from one another.

Another important element of the mentoring I received from Pop was the safe space he provided for me to formulate my own beliefs. Since Pop was such a quiet man, we had few, if any, conversations about our respective beliefs about religion or most anything else. Even though he was a strong New York Giants baseball fan long before they moved to San Francisco, and I was a strong St. Louis Cardinals fan because Stan "the Man" Musial was my boyhood hero (which did not make life easy for me in Brooklyn when the LA Dodgers were the Brooklyn Dodgers), Pop and I didn't even talk about the relative strengths of our two teams. We just enjoyed going to the old Polo Grounds together, along with my brother, to watch whomever was in town to play the Giants.

Some would see this paucity of conversations about beliefs as a shortcoming in my upbringing. Although, in retrospect, I now wish that Pop and I had had some more conversations, the fact that Pop didn't coerce me to believe exactly as he did proved to be a gift, especially when I compare it with the rebellion that sometimes emerges when young people are raised in doctrinaire homes where they are not provided with safe and welcoming spaces to shape their own beliefs—or, if not outright rebellion, the stunted growth that results when you are expected to live out a set of hand-me-down beliefs rather than having a safe space to think for yourself and formulate your own.[7]

In summary, although there were some bumps in the road due to differences in beliefs about religion between Mom and Pop, the kindness and gentleness they exemplified is what had the most lasting impact on the life ahead of me.

7. A novel that beautifully captures the importance of formulating your own set of beliefs to live by is *The Chosen* by Chaim Potok. This story is about some Jewish kids from Brooklyn who couldn't accept the totality of beliefs that their parents and others in the Jewish tradition embraced, but didn't want to reject that rich tradition. Rather, they needed to find an expression of the Jewish tradition that they could completely embrace and live by. I devoured the pages of that book, since I was a Christian kid from Brooklyn who had a similar struggle.

CHAPTER 6

Lessons Learned and Questions for Conversation

Up to this point, I have shared the ways in which elements in my story, especially my engagements with a number of mentors, have informed my evolving understanding of what it means to be a follower of Jesus.

I've tried to show that my experience of listening well to Christians from different Christian traditions and different personal backgrounds has both deepened and broadened my understanding of what it means to be a follower of Jesus. It's taught me I should never silence someone who disagrees with me; I should always provide a safe and welcoming space to express and talk respectfully about our disagreements.

In the next three chapters, I will seek to draw out the implications of what you have read so far in the following three stages:

- Some lessons I have learned along the way and some meddlesome questions begging for further conversation (this chapter)

- A report on my recent efforts to put into practice what I have learned along the way, including what has worked well and what has failed miserably (ch. 7)

- My proposal for orchestrating more inclusive conversations within individual churches to bridge existing dividing lines among followers of Jesus (ch. 8)

Lessons Learned

No Christian Tradition Has the Corner on God's Truth

My own in-depth immersion in three Christian traditions (Pietist Lutheran, Reformed, and Anabaptist/Mennonite) has made an important contribution to my understanding of what it means to be a faithful follower of Jesus. But the truths I have gleaned from each tradition have been partial (truncated), needing to be complemented by insights from other traditions.

Exposure to Theological Otherness Is Vital

If no Christian tradition has the corner on God's truth, it is very important for Christians who wish to develop a full-orbed view of what it means to be a follower of Jesus to familiarize themselves with the best insights of theological traditions other than their own.

This is not to suggest that adherents to a particular Christian tradition should diminish their attempts to continuously draw out implications from their respective traditions about how best to be a follower of Jesus. But it does suggest they should also be in conversation with adherents from other traditions who could provide insights that complement, enrich, and maybe even, at times, correct the insights of their home traditions.

Conversations with Those in Other Christian Traditions Will Reveal That They Are Also Deeply Committed Christians

It was only when I dared to go outside of my comfort zone by engaging in conversations with Christians outside of the Pietist Lutheran tradition of my upbringing (especially some of my mentors) that I discovered they too had a deep commitment to be faithful followers of Jesus and had much to teach me about the contours of such faithfulness that were not prominent in my own tradition.

The First Rule for Conversation Is to Listen Well

When you see, in person, the deep Christian commitment of those outside of your own tradition, you will want to learn from those Christians. And the best way to start that learning process is to listen well, to make sure that you fully understand the beliefs of the other and her reasons for holding to those beliefs. Due to her own unique personal biography and other aspects of her social location, she may be able to provide insights you have missed. As you get to know one another better, building personal relationships of mutual understanding and trust, she is likely to reciprocate, listening carefully to you and learning from the insights you have gleaned from your unique personal biography.

Listening Well and Then Talking Respectfully about Agreements and Disagreements Is a Deep Expression of Love

I have not come across any Christian who denies that Jesus taught all who aspire to be his followers to love others (Matt 22:39). But there is great diversity in how Christians believe they should express such love.

Based primarily on my own painful experience of being silenced when I was treated unjustly while having to depart Messiah College, I have reached the hard-earned conclusion that you don't love someone whom you have silenced. Stated positively, to provide someone who disagrees with you a safe and welcoming space to express that disagreement and then to talk respectfully about your disagreement is a deep expression of love—an expression of love that is all too often neglected or, worse yet, violated by many Christians.

Dig Down Deep to Christian Values

Recall that thanks to the mentoring of David Wolfe I have placed great importance on posing questions about values (axiological questions). This is based on my belief that if you dig beneath the surface of any decision, you will uncover one or more value commitments.

This suggests that when a Christian is contemplating any decision, including choosing a position on an issue, he or she should dig deep down to identify the Christian values that are at stake. My experience suggests that all too often we Christians base our decisions, including taking positions on contentious issues, on values we have absorbed from our broader culture, which may be antithetical to fundamental Christian values. I will offer one concrete example.

I recently co-facilitated a small-group conversation in an adult discipleship class at my home church in Iowa on the topic "Christian Perspectives on News Headlines." We were talking about one of the four pillars in President Trump's position on immigration, the pillar that seeks to limit chain migration. As I listened to the opinions expressed by those attending this class, both Republicans and Democrats, I discovered that each participant was essentially echoing the party line. I called for a time out, reminding my class attendees, "I didn't ask you what your political party says about this issue. I asked you to present your 'Christian perspective' on this issue based on your understanding of foundational Christian values." The subsequent conversation improved somewhat. But it was a constant challenge to get the attendees to dare to be critical of the perspectives embraced by their particular political parties. It is a grave error to assume that the values embraced by either major political are necessarily congruent with Christian values.

Therefore, here are two more words of advice for your consideration:

If you ever have the opportunity to facilitate a group conversation on any contentious issue (political or otherwise) in any setting (in church, in school, or around the family dinner table), push your conversation partners to dig down deep to their Christian value commitments as the basis on which they stake their positions.

For every choice you make in life, base your decision on your understanding of foundational Christian values.

I have tried, not always successfully, to live by the second word of advice offered above. In particular, I try to exemplify:

- The Christian virtues of the fruit of the Spirit (love, joy, peace, patience, kindness, generosity, faithfulness, gentleness, self-control) and other enduring attitudes such as humility, courage, patience, and hope.

- Christian values that reflect my understanding of God's redemptive purposes for all of creation, such as seeking the truth about all aspects of God's creation; showing concern for the well-being of others, with a special focus on doing justice for the poor and marginalized amongst us; helping to bring about peace and reconciliation between persons and groups in conflict; fostering the redemption of broken systemic structures in society; caring for the natural world that God has created; and creating beauty.

There is a synergy between these two sets of Christian values. Since I can't do everything and since my enduring attitudes have a significant influence on what I believe I should do at any given time, the extent to which I possess the Christian virtues in the first set of values will inform decision-making about Christian value(s) in the second set I will seek to foster, taking into account my perception of my particular giftedness.

I have shared the above lessons learned with many Christians through an ongoing Respectful Conversation Project (that I will report on in the next chapter), from which some encouraging results have emerged. But I generally feel like a voice crying in the wilderness because I have found all too few Christians who share the commitments expressed in these lessons. Why is that?

Questions for Conversation

I will attempt to get you to think about a possible response to that question by posing a few meddlesome subquestions.

Have Christians Succumbed to the Scourge of Tribalism?

It has been persuasively argued that the primary cause for the current high degree of polarization and fragmentation in American society today is tribalism—an us-versus-them mentality that holds that "my group" has the truth, the whole truth, and nothing but the truth about the issue at hand, and that those persons in "that other group" who disagree possess little, if any, of that truth.

In its most pernicious form, these tribalists believe that because those other folks are completely wrong, they are evil and need to be demonized. Those "other folks" can be those who attend another church, those who worship in another religious tradition, those who claim no religious commitment, or, in the political realm, those who belong to the other political party. As Kevin den Dulk has pointed out, such polarization is primarily "affective" in that it reflects a deep emotional attachment to your tribe.[1]

According to this way of thinking, outside of trying to convert someone to accept your beliefs, there is really no point in even talking to the members of another tribe about your disagreements. They have absolutely nothing to teach you.

As much as we Christians and others may bemoan such rampant tribalism, we need to ask ourselves whether we are part of the problem. If we refuse to listen to and talk respectfully with those from other Christian traditions who disagree with us, we may be succumbing to the scourge of tribalism. And if we believe that we have the whole truth about the issue at hand, we eliminate the possibility of gaining a more comprehensive perspective that can enrich a truncated view.

Why have so many Christians succumbed to the scourge of tribalism, and how can such tribalism be overcome? We tend toward tribalism when we live in insulated Christian communities without engaging deeply committed Christians who have differing beliefs about what it means to be a faithful follower of Jesus. We can break out of such tribalism only by stepping out of our comfort zones by engaging in more inclusive respectful conversations with

1. Heie, *Reforming American Politics,* 141–42.

those other Christians, creating the potential for us to learn much from each other.

Have Some Christians Submerged or Marginalized Other Christian Traditions to Maintain Prominence and Power?

This is perhaps the most meddlesome question that I pose for our collective consideration. Catherine Brekus and Clark Gilpin suggest that a desire to maintain prominence and power has often been operative throughout the history of Christianity.

> The predominant Christian groups of each era have tried to submerge or marginalize alternative visions of Christianity in order to stake a claim to their own orthodoxy, centrality, and power.[2]

Do we Christians avoid engaging those from other Christian traditions or those who hold differing beliefs out of fear that if they are given a voice, the result could be a diminishment of our tradition, our particular beliefs, the respectability or prestige (or financial support) our Christian organization enjoys, or the applause we crave?

Some prominent Christian leaders have been critical of my advocacy for giving a voice to everyone and creating a safe and welcoming space for disagreement about contentious issues. In a few conversations I have had with such leaders, I have been saddened by a pattern in responses that in effect asks, "What will our constituents or supporters think if they find out we are even talking about such a controversial issue?" Is such a response guided more by adherence to values such as cultural acceptance, admiration, prestige, and power than commitment to foundational Christian values like love, humility, courage, and the quest for truth? I respectfully suggest that these prominent Christian leaders failed to dig down deep to foundational Christian values.

To generalize, we Christians must confess to our tendency to uncritically embrace prominent American cultural values that

2. Brekus and Gilpin, *American Christianities*, 4.

are antithetical to the Christian faith. As suggested in the "Lessons Learned" above, we must always dig down deep to Christian values as we seek to be faithful followers of Jesus.

Is the Root Problem a Lack of Humility That Fails to Combine Commitment and Openness?

As I have tried to illustrate from selected aspects of my own story, elements of my personal biography deeply inform my beliefs, as do other elements of my social location, such as my gender, race, sexual orientation, and socioeconomic status. The beliefs of someone who disagrees with me about a given issue may be deeply informed by her differing set of particularities that may enable her to see things that I miss, just as my unique particularities may enable me to see things that she misses. And since we are both finite and fallible human beings, we cannot claim that either of our partial glimpses captures the full truth on the matter, as only fully understood by God. In addition, I can be blinded when I succumb to the temptation to sin by thinking it's all about me and those who agree with me. As Scripture teaches, we all "see in a mirror, dimly" (1 Cor 13:12).

It is hubris—a gross failure to exemplify an appropriate attitude of humility—for me to assume that I have a God's-eye view of the truth about the issue at hand. It takes genuine humility for me to express my beliefs with clarity and conviction while acknowledging that the contrary beliefs of another person may help me to refine my beliefs, possibly improving them or even correcting them.

Note that such humility does not mean being wishy-washy about your beliefs. Rather, it involves holding in tension that very rare combination of embracing and expressing your beliefs with clarity and deep conviction while also acknowledging that you have only a partial view of the whole truth and you may even be wrong about some things.

Both Ian Barbour and Richard Mouw have given eloquent expression to the nature of this rare combination. In his book *Myths,*

Models, and Paradigms, Barbour proposes the following definition of religious maturity:

> It is by no means easy to hold beliefs for which you would be willing to die, and yet to remain open to new insights. But it is precisely such a combination of commitment and inquiry that constitutes religious maturity.[3]

In his splendid book, *Uncommon Decency,* Richard Mouw draws on Martin Marty to highlight the importance of civility in living out this rare combination of commitment and inquiry, calling for a convicted civility.

> One of the real problems in modern life is that the people who are good at being civil often lack strong convictions and people who have strong convictions often lack civility.... We need to find a way of combining a civil outlook with a "passionate intensity" about our convictions. The real challenge is to come up with a *convicted civility.*[4]

Openness to the beliefs of others without commitment to your own beliefs too easily leads to sheer relativism (I have my beliefs, you have yours, end of conversation). Commitment to your own beliefs without openness to listening to and carefully considering the contrary beliefs of others too easily leads to fanaticism, even terrorism. (As C. S. Lewis has observed, and what past and current world events tragically testify, "Those who are readiest to die for a cause may easily become those who are readiest to kill for it."[5]) *One of the most pressing needs in our world today is for all human beings, whatever their religious or secular faith commitments, to embrace and hold in tension both commitment and openness, giving living expression to "convicted civility."*

Do we Christians avoid engaging those from other Christian traditions or those who hold differing beliefs about a given issue because we lack humility? There is a way forward only if Christian communities can identify members of their communities who

3. Barbour, *Myths, Models, and Paradigms,* 136.

4. Mouw, *Uncommon Decency,* 12 (emphasis original).

5. Lewis, *Reflections on the Psalms,* 28.

embrace that rare combination of deep commitment to their own beliefs with openness to respectfully listen to and then talk with other Christians who are deeply committed to a differing set of beliefs.

CHAPTER 7

Planting Tiny Seeds
of Redemptive Conversation

During the last ten years, I have attempted to put into practice
the lessons I wrote about in the last chapter. What follows is
my story about what led up to those initiatives with which I am still
involved, as well as a summary description of their contours. The
successes, as well as one big flop, have deeply informed my recommendations for orchestrating more inclusive conversations within
individual churches, which I'll share in the concluding chapter.

Since I was fired from my VPAA position at Messiah College
in August of 1993, after I had signed a contract for the 1993–94 academic year, the college was obligated to pay me for that year (what
some of my faculty friends at Messiah jokingly called the "Harold
Heie sabbatical year").

It afforded me time to explore various possibilities for future
employment, including applying for presidency positions at three
CCCU schools. I made it to the final four at all three colleges, but
during the course of my interviews, it became apparent that these
colleges were looking primarily for a fundraiser and public rela-
tions type, so my enthusiastic assertion that as president I would
focus on strengthening the college's commitment to the integration
of faith and learning seemed to fall on deaf ears. I received no offers to assume a college presidency. In retrospect, if I had received
and accepted such an offer, it would surely have led to a whopping

exemplification of being promoted to my level of incompetency (the Peter Principle).

In the spring of 1994, with an offer in hand for a VPAA position at a Christian college in Colorado, I received a phone call from my good friend of many years, Stan Gaede, then provost at Gordon College, where Stan and I had been teaching colleagues in the late 1970s. Stan had a dream for Gordon that was among the approved initiatives of a long-range plan, and he was looking for someone to help him shape and implement that dream. His exact words were: "Harold, Gordon just approved a long-range plan that calls for the establishment of a center to promote 'Christian thought and action.' Would you be interested in serving as the founding director of that center?"

Would I be interested? Is the pope Catholic? Does a bear relieve himself in the woods? Another instance of the dynamism of my attempts to be a faithful follower of Jesus was emerging. During my VPAA stints at Northwestern College and Messiah College, I had come to embrace the importance of enabling faculty to be productive scholars as an essential part of being effective teachers. Since the Gordon board mandate was so succinct, I would have the opportunity to flesh it out, in conversation with Stan, in ways that would enable Gordon faculty to do more scholarly work.

Furthermore, I could shape the programming of this new center in ways that built on the collaborative vision for leadership that had emerged in my VPAA stints, with increased emphasis on the importance of a leader listening well to his or her followers.

A catch was that Gordon didn't have the resources to adequately fund this new center; they had just enough for a modest operating budget and a half-time salary. I would have to raise external funds from foundations and private philanthropists to pay for the other half of my salary, a salary for an administrative assistant, and the costs for all the center's programming initiatives. It was the best job offer I have ever received.

Stan and I enthusiastically collaborated in shaping this new center, which we called the Center for Christian Studies (it has been renamed the Center for Faith and Inquiry). To explore potential programming, I repeated the listening tour that I first used when I became VPAA at Northwestern. I invited interested Gordon faculty members to sit down with me over coffee or lunch to tell me about their dreams for future scholarly work. I then fleshed out their aspirations in the form of grant proposals, which typically included collaboration between the Gordon faculty member and Christian scholars elsewhere who shared the same research interest.

Because the research interests of Gordon faculty were quite varied, the topics for which I was able to garner external funding (about $3 million total) during my tenure at the CCS (1994–2003) were all over the map, including global stewardship, Christian apologetics, civic education, Christian virtues in a pluralistic society, and evangelical hermeneutics. The culmination of each research project was to bring the team of participating Christian scholars to the Gordon campus to listen to and discuss each other's reports on their respective scholarly contributions to the overall project. These positive experiences further reinforced my perception of my giftedness that had been evolving over many years: I am best at helping others to do their best.

In addition to these CCS research projects based on the interest of individual Gordon faculty members, the CCS also hosted a number of public forums that brought together, for listening and conversation, scholars and practitioners who had strong disagreements about hot-button issues. These included a colloquium at historic Faneuil Hall in Boston around the theme "International Public Policy"; an interfaith dialogue, co-hosted with the American Jewish Committee, that brought together Jewish and Christian scholars and public leaders to discuss "The Role of Religion in Politics and Society"; and a seminar series in which Protestant and Catholic laypersons discussed the theme "Unity, Not Uniformity."

My Respectful Conversation Project

After I retired (sort of) in 2003, and moved back to Orange City, Iowa, I further built on my positive CCS experiences fostering conversations among Christians and others who have strong disagreements by initiating a huge Respectful Conversation Project on a website, respectfulconversation.net.

I was prompted to initiate my Respectful Conversation Project by my dismay at the dismal state of public discourse in America, particularly on social media. There had to be a better way, a Christian way, for Christians and others who disagree to engage each other about their disagreements—a way that goes beyond the scourge of tribalism and the demonization of those who disagree.

Simply put, the purpose of my website is to model a way to navigate our many disagreements that is deeply informed by Christian values. Interested readers can access all the details of my Respectful Conversation Project on my website, which includes a blog (my musings) and four major electronic conversations (eCircles) that I have hosted over the past ten years.

Each of my eCircles lasted from eight to ten months and was followed by my publication of a book presenting the highlights of the postings. The topics for my eCircles and the resulting books were as follows:

- Alternative Political Conversation, published as *Evangelicals on Public Policy Issues: Sustaining a Respectful Political Conversation*
- American Evangelicalism, published as *A Future for American Evangelicalism: Commitment, Openness, and Conversation*
- Human Sexuality, published as *Respectful LGBT Conversations: Seeking Truth, Giving Love, and Modeling Christian Unity*
- Reforming Political Discourse, published as *Reforming American Politics: A Christian Perspective on Moving Past Conflict to Conversation*

For each eCircle, I first enlisted the assistance of a consultant who had proven competence relative to the given theme. The consultant then helped me identify pertinent subtopics and a leading question or two to be posed for each subtopic. For example, here are the first three (of nine) subtopics and leading questions for my human sexuality eCircle.[1]

1. Voices from the Gay Community
   Leading question: What are your beliefs about morally appropriate relationships between persons who experience same-sex attraction?

2. Biblical Understandings
   Leading question: What is your understanding of biblical/theological teachings relevant to issues being raised by Christians who identify themselves as members of the LGBT community?

3. Findings from the Academic Disciplines
   Leading question: What is your understanding of the best findings from the academic disciplines of biology, anthropology, psychology, and sociology relative to same-sex attraction, sexual orientation, and sexual behavior for human beings?

For each eCircle, I spent a considerable amount of time (two to three months of about half-time work) identifying conversation partners for each subtopic (generally two in number) whom I knew would have significant disagreements in their responses to the leading question(s) and who would agree, up front, to abide by the following "Guidelines for Respectful Conversation":

- I will try to listen well, providing each person with a welcoming space to express her perspective on the issue at hand.

- I will seek to empathetically understand the reasons another person has for her perspective.

- I will express my perspective and my reasons for holding that perspective, with clarity and conviction, but with a noncoercive style that invites conversation with a person who disagrees with me.

- In my conversation with a person who disagrees with me, I will explore whether we can find some common ground that

1. My very capable consultant for this eCircle was Julia Stronks, professor of political science at Whitworth University, Washington.

can further the conversation. But if we cannot find common ground, I will conclude that we can only agree to disagree, doing so in a way that demonstrates respect for the other and concern for her well-being and does not foreclose the possibility of future conversations.

- In aspiring to these ideals for conversation, I will also aspire to be characterized by humility, courage, patience, and love.

It is important, for future reference in this book, for me to report on the great difficulty I had recruiting conversation partners for my four eCircles and to reflect on possible reasons for that difficulty. The average pattern for a given subtopic was that the ratio of invitations I extended to acceptances received was about five to one (e.g., one hundred invitations extended to recruit twenty conversation partners).

Why was that? The responses from most of those invitees who rejected my invitation was that "they were too busy." I can certainly understand that response since I have often felt like I was too busy. But since I have never been too busy to do something that I thought was really important, I cannot help but wonder out loud about how those who rejected my invitations would have responded to two follow-up questions that I now wish I had asked:

- Did you feel uncomfortable with the "Guidelines for Respectful Conversation" you were expected to agree to?

- Are your responses to my leading questions so set in stone that you see little value in listening to and talking with those who disagree with you?

Alas, I have no idea as to how those who rejected my invitations would have responded to these follow-up questions. But I am confident that those who accepted my invitations shared my conviction that agreement to abide by my conversation guidelines was a necessary precondition for a productive dialogue—and that they embraced that rare combination of commitment to their own beliefs and openness to listening to and seriously considering the contrary beliefs of others that is a precondition for a productive dialogue. After a description of how these conversations were implemented, I will point to evidence that the ensuing conversations were both respectful and productive in the sense of helping to uncover some areas of agreement and illuminating remaining areas of disagreement sufficient to inform ongoing conversation.

For each eCircle, a month was devoted to each subtopic. During that month, each conversation partner was asked to post three 3,000-to-4,000-word postings with the following foci:

- The first of the month: Your response to the leading question(s)
- The tenth: Your identification of agreements and disagreements with the first postings
- The twentieth: Your perception of unresolved issues that call for ongoing conversation

For those readers of this book who are not faint of heart, you can judge how well (or not) these conversations went by reading either the complete compilation of postings on my website or the four books that eventually emerged. My own evaluation is that the conversation partners for each of these eCircles exemplified respectful conversations about disagreements to an admirable degree, the result of which was that they were able to identify areas of agreement and illuminate remaining areas of disagreement sufficient to lay the foundation for ongoing conversation.

The following testimony of appreciation from Justin Lee for the conversation he had with Eve Tushnet on the subtopic "Voices from the Gay Community" warmed my heart. (Justin is a gay Christian who believes that God will bless same-sex marriages based on lifelong covenantal commitments; Eve is a gay Christian who believes that gay Christians are called to lives of celibacy.)

> So as I wrap up my part in this conversation, I find myself deeply moved. I am moved by Eve's grace in disagreement and her friendship to me as we challenge one another. I am encouraged, too, by the depth of conversation we've been able to have in six simple articles. But I'm also reminded why these conversations are so important in the first place. Many hurting, lonely people's lives hang in the balance.

My own position on this topic hasn't changed, but my appreciation for Eve and understanding of her view has certainly increased, and I'd say that's worth it. Respectful conversation of this sort is hugely undervalued in the church. It may not always change minds, but it is powerful and effective. Given the importance of this topic, we can't afford *not* to listen to each other.

We are, after all, supposed to be known by our love.

For future reference, I believe that one of the reasons why some agreements were uncovered in my eCircles is that after each first posting, the conversation partners were given ten days to review and think about the posting before responding to identify areas of agreement and disagreement. The tendency in face-to-face conversations is to want to talk about agreements and disagreements immediately, thus not giving each conversation partner adequate time for reflection. As you will eventually see in my chapter 8 recommendations for orchestrating more inclusive conversations within individual churches, I will suggest a way to avoid this problem when hosting face-to-face conversations.

A Face-to-Face Conversation on LGBT Issues That Failed

Buoyed by the positive results that emerged from my four eCircles, I decided to pivot and focus my next attempts at orchestrating respectful conversations on hosting small-group face-to-face conversations in the northwest Iowa community where I now live.

Shortly after my book on LGBT issues that sought to capture the highlights of my eCircle on human sexuality was released,[2] I offered to teach an adult discipleship class at my home church (American Reformed Church in Orange City) to be devoted to discussing the content of my book.

As we do for all adult discipleship classes offered at my church, I extended an open-ended general invitation to all church members to attend my class. Only four members expressed interest:

2. Heie, *Respectful LGBT Conversations*.

a married lesbian couple, a member who leans toward affirming same-sex marriages, and a member who said she was "confused." No one who opposed same-sex marriage expressed an interest in attending.

Despite the low numbers, I offered the class, adding two attendees from a local Episcopal church whom I knew would be respectful conversation partners (who also supported same-sex marriage). We spent our first two sessions talking about the purpose of our class, which was *not* to win an argument but to better understand each other's positions and the reasons for holding those positions and to agree to abide by the "Guidelines for Respectful Conversation" (shared above) that would inform how we listened to and talked to one another.

By the end of our second session together, it was painfully obvious that two things were missing: The first was voices of those who opposed same-sex marriage. Therefore, before our third session, I recruited a good friend of mine from my church whom I knew opposed same-sex marriage and he, in turn, recruited a friend of his from another local church who vehemently opposed same-sex marriage.

A second missing element in the composition of my small group were the voices of those Christian scholars having expertise in various academic disciplines relative to same-sex attraction and sexual orientation. Group members were anxious to share their biblical understandings regarding these two challenging issues. But, as I argued in chapter 3, it is important to integrate biblical understanding with adequate understanding of findings in the various academic disciplines and to seek connections between these two areas of knowledge.

We continued to meet for another few sessions. But it soon became obvious that not all participants were willing to *both* express their beliefs about human sexuality with deep conviction *and* be open to seriously considering alternative beliefs. (This was due in part, I believe, to the fact that not all participants were at the first two sessions where attendees agreed to the importance of exemplifying that rare combination).

In retrospect, I made some huge mistakes in this my first attempt to orchestrate a respectful face-to-face conversation about a contentious issue. Most notably, I should not have extended a general invitation to attend this class to my entire church family, hoping, very naively, that those deciding to attend would reflect a "balance" of competing beliefs about same-sex marriage. And my attempt to create such a balance by adding conversation partners after our second session was also a huge blunder, since those added had not been present in our first two sessions when we agreed on the rules for our conversation.

Hopefully, in my concrete proposal in the next chapter for a way forward, you will see how I have learned from my mistakes.

My Trump Conversation

I am persistent (and patient). After my first failed attempt at orchestrating a fruitful face-to-face conversation about human sexuality, I decided to really walk into a den of lions by initiating a face-to-face conversation on the topic "President Trump and Visions for America." That initiative also did not start well, but it ended well, in my estimation.[3]

The reason this initiative did not start well is that I had not yet learned my lesson regarding achieving the right balance of select invitees. So I extended a general invitation to participate in a piece that I wrote for a local newspaper.

The silence was deafening. For quite a while, I received no responses to my invitation. But then I received a lone response from a local resident who said he was a strong supporter of President Trump, but he was interested in listening to and talking with other local residents who did not support Trump. Bingo! I found someone who exemplified that rare combination of commitment and

---

3. For a complete account of the eleven sessions for this conversation and my final report focusing on the areas of agreement and disagreement that emerged, unanswered questions that beg for ongoing conversation, and my advice for those who wish to replicate this experiment, go to respectfulconversation.net.

openness that is an unyielding precondition for having a respectful conversation.

So, consistent with my lifelong practice of first trying to listen well, he and I met for coffee and talked about how to proceed. To make a long story short, we decided to individually recruit local residents we knew personally toward a goal of ending up with a cohort of eight conversation partners: four (including him) who identify themselves as generally supporters of President Trump and four who identify themselves as generally nonsupporters of President Trump. (The qualifier "generally" reflects the fact that none of these eight conversations partners agreed or disagreed with everything President Trump said or did.)

I once again started this face-to-face conversation with two sessions devoted to talking about the purpose of our conversation—what we hope to get out of it—and to understanding and agreeing to abide by the "Guidelines for Respectful Conversation" enumerated above. After these initial sessions focusing on getting to know one another, the eight conversation partners (with me serving as moderator) launched into sharing their respective visions for America and their views about the extent to which President Trump was, or was not, accomplishing their respective visions. The remainder of our conversation focused on seeking to identify areas of agreement and areas of disagreement.

A number of areas of agreement emerged, such as consensus that current political discourse is broken, respectful conversation is an antidote to this brokenness, and the place to start a respectful conversation about political disagreement is to get to know the person who disagrees with you before launching into expressing your disagreements.

My conversation partners also agreed that "listening well" toward the goal of seeking mutual understanding was crucial. But here I detected a difference between what I call weak and strong forms of listening.

In brief, a weak view of listening just involves being polite—letting the other person talk without interruption, but without giving serious consideration to the possible validity of what the other person is saying. In stark contrast, a strong view of listening involves a willingness to seriously consider the contrary beliefs of others and a willingness to critically examine your own beliefs in light of these contrary beliefs. I believe it is fair to say that at various times, my conversation partners gave evidence of both weak and strong forms of listening. The rarity of the combination of commitment to one's own beliefs and genuine openness to seriously considering the differing beliefs of others became all too apparent.

Other areas of agreement that emerged were that no one seemed to have changed their minds about the presidency of Donald Trump, but some of the conversation partners noted ways in which they changed during the course of the conversations (e.g., "I have become less disagreeable"; "I have increased my capacity to listen, desire to understand, and ability to love those who disagree with me").

Especially important was general agreement that "my perception of the other conversation partners changed," dispelling any initial impressions there may have been that those who disagree with me about political issues are inferior Christians. One quote from conversation partner Steve Mahr captures this most eloquently:

> One thing that I feel has emerged from this [conversation] . . . is that I think we all see each other as part of the same 'Christian family.' . . . I think some of us feel like really distantly related cousins, but I think we see in one another a genuine love of Christ and an authentic desire to follow Jesus. And really, I'm not sure I could want more than that from a conversation. To be able to see one another as co-citizens of the kingdom of God is a great conclusion to any conversation if you ask me.

I highlight this beautiful quote because this change in perception about those who had (and still have) some strong disagreements is no small accomplishment.[4] Since the conclusion of this

---

4. The Mennonite scholar Carolyn Schrock-Shenk captured the significance of this accomplishment in the following observation about what makes a dialogue genuine: "What exactly makes dialogue genuine? Does one need to be open to changing one's perspective or conviction about an issue? In my view, that readiness to change is the ideal but it is rarely realistic . . . I have come to believe that a minimum requirement for genuine dialogue is a readiness to

Trump conversation, I now believe that it is the most important accomplishment of our experiment. This reflection also fits extremely well with the overarching purpose of this book since it points to the priority of first building personal relationships of mutual understanding and trust as a foundation for then seeking to identify some common ground.

The areas of disagreement that were not resolved during our conversations are hinted at by eleven unanswered questions enumerated in my final online report, which included the following three questions, all of which were related to disagreements about the scope of the government's role: "What is the relationship between the call for Christians to address the needs of the poor and marginalized in society and the possible role of government in addressing such needs?"; "Are the needs of the poor and marginalized in our society too extensive to be met solely by means of private charity?"; and "Is the call to address the needs of the poor and marginalized in our society just a Christian calling, or is it a calling to be embraced by all human beings?"

Two procedural recommendations emerged from our conversations that could be of help to those who may wish to replicate our experiment in their spheres of influence (further elaboration is contained in my final online report).

First, great care must be taken in formulating the leading questions to which conversation partners respond. In my Trump conversation, I started with rather general questions about each conversation partner's vison for America and the extent to which President Trump is facilitating that vision. It soon became apparent that some of the conversation partners would have preferred to talk about some of President Trump's policy initiatives (e.g., on taxes and immigration). In retrospect, I should have asked the conversation partners for their input about what they consider to be the most pressing questions prior to finalizing my leading questions. I should also have called on the expertise of consultants, as I did for my various online conversations, especially to help me to formulate some questions to ensure that the conversation partners, most of

---

change or modify one's perspective about the *person or persons* holding the opposite point of view" (Schrock-Shenk, "Foreword," 15).

whom were lay persons, would give serious consideration to per-spectives from members of the Christian academy.

My second rather unusual procedural recommendation flows from a significant difference that emerged in the extent to which common ground (areas of agreement) emerged in this face-to-face Trump conversation (not as extensive as I had hoped) and the more significant extent to which common ground emerged in the various online conversations I have hosted on my website over recent years (reported on earlier in this chapter). Let me explain.

In my previous online conversations, I typically had just two conversation partners for a given subtopic (usually responding to one leading question that I posed). By means of three succes-sive postings during a given month, these two conversation part-ners had ample opportunity to identify areas of agreement and disagreement.

In contrast, in my face-to-face Trump conversation, having eight conversation partners led to such a cacophony of differing responses to a given leading question that it was much harder to pin down areas of agreement and disagreement. This suggests the rather novel possibility of a procedural variation on our experiment that pairs conversation partners to discuss a given leading ques-tion. Each pairing then reports back to the entire group the results of their attempts to find some common ground as good prepara-tion for the attempt of the larger group to identify some common ground.

To set a context for a concluding reflection on what I would have done differently if I could moderate this Trump conversation all over again, here is my summary of the highlights of what I report above.

- We did it! Although our bold experiment was far from perfect, we did create something that is extremely rare these days in our polarized society characterized too often by a tribalistic us-versus-them mentality: We successfully created a safe and welcoming space to express and talk respectfully about dis-agreements. This is a major accomplishment.

- Respectful conversations among Christians who have strong disagreements about the Trump presidency can significantly change perceptions about the Christian commitment of those who disagree with you: they are not inferior Christians, they are brothers and sisters in Christ who have reasons for their differing views based on their understanding of Christian values. This is another major accomplishment.

- This Trump conversation did not significantly change the views of my conversation partners about the extent to which President Trump does, or does not, speak or act in accordance with Christian values.

- In my estimation, there were mixed results on the question of weak vs. strong listening. It seemed that sometimes conversation partners just listened politely to those who disagreed with them rather than critically examining their own views in light of the contrary views of others.

The last two bullets[5] above hint at the possibility that the reason this conversation did not change the minds of the conversation partners about the Trump presidency was that they settled for politeness, without adequately examining their own views in light of the contrary views of others. I suspect this was the case.

Assuming so, if I could moderate this conversation all over again, I would revise the "Guidelines for Respectful Conversation" that we all agreed upon, as enumerated in the "My Respectful Conversation Project" section above, to include the following guideline:

In my conversation with a person who disagrees with me, I will explore whether we can find some common ground by critically examining my own view in light of her contrary view and the reasons she has for her view.

This change will lead to a revised set of the five guidelines that I will present in the next chapter.

---

5. Some of my Mennonite friends jokingly express preference for the word "pearls" over "bullets."

An Old Lesson Learned in a New Way: The Importance of Listening to the Stories of Others

By now, it should be apparent that an important aspect of my commitment to listening well to others, especially those who disagree with me, is to listen carefully to their stories, since what they believe to be true is often deeply informed by what they have experienced in their personal pilgrimages.

The truth of this observation was brought home to me once again about eight years ago during one of the sessions in an adult discipleship class for which I was providing leadership at my home church in Orange City, Iowa. This series was devoted to the topic of immigration. In planning this series, we made the wise decision that we would not be talking *about* our new immigrant neighbors, but *with* them.

So during one of our sessions, a Latino mother told all of us her heartbreaking story of how each morning before leaving for school, her daughter would be in tears because of her fear that when she returned home from school her undocumented mommy would be gone, having been taken away by ICE for deportation.

Hearing that story broke my heart and had a huge impact on my life. Until I heard that story, my new Latino immigrant neighbors were mostly abstractions, mere statistics. Now I fully realized that they were real live flesh-and-blood human beings who were hurting deeply and needed my help. I had made a human connection. This observation is consistent with the assertion from Arthur Brooks that "to understand others and help them understand us, we must have a human connection, and the way to do this is through stories."[6]

The lesson that was especially brought home to me that night (not a new lesson, since it lies behind much of my story I have already told) is captured in the following word of advice:

Go out of your way to get to know those around you by listening to the stories of their lives; it will help you to discern ways in which you can help them to flourish.

6. Brooks, *Love Your Enemies*, 148–49.

It was primarily because of the impact of this story that I decided to add to the redemptive seeds I wanted to sow and work on behalf of CASA (Center for Assistance, Service and Advocacy) of Sioux County—an organization for which I have served as co-director.[7]

My Work Trying to Help My New Latino Neighbors to Flourish

The vision of CASA of Sioux County is for "transformed northwest Iowa communities that welcome, empower, and celebrate people from all cultures." Space limitations in this book do not allow me to elaborate much on our various initiatives to foster this vision, especially for our growing number of new Latino neighbors in Sioux County. (Interested readers can go to casasiouxcounty.org for elaboration.)[8]

Here I will only mention one CASA initiative we have pursued for many years—advocating for comprehensive immigration reform—since this is related to the conversational model for Christians doing politics that I proposed in chapter 4.

We have had face-to-face meetings with our former US House representative Steve King, who is notorious for his vilification of undocumented immigrants; Senator Chuck Grassley; and

7. Adding my work with CASA to my various initiatives for orchestrating respectful conversations gives new meaning to the word "retirement." I am as busy, if not more so, than I was before retiring, a big difference being that I no longer get paid. But that is okay since as a card-carrying workaholic, I love being busy and I am no good at shuffleboard. For those readers anticipating retirement, the really good news is that you get to pick and choose those projects that fit best with your understanding of how you can continue partnering with God by planting tiny seeds of redemption.

8. In an article in the June 2020 issue of *Sojourners* magazine, Matt Hildreth (a former colleague of mine at CASA) asserts that what is working in Sioux County as an antidote to the toxic polarization and demonization prevalent in national politics is that leaders there have rooted their efforts in authentic relationships and dialogue, citing the Respectful Conversation Project on my website as taking this idea to a new level (which warms my heart). I believe it is fair to say that the work of CASA has been based on commitment to establishing authentic personal relationships and engaging in respectful dialogue.

a number of local elected Iowa politicians. It has mostly been like talking to the wind because of the impasse between those holding to the "conservative" position that those who have broken the law by entering the USA without documentation should be penalized by means of deportation and those holding to the "liberal" position that the biblical call to welcome the stranger means that the undocumented immigrants among us should be provided a pathway to citizenship. As I suggest in chapter 4, that is a false either/or choice. As the "gang of eight" legislators demonstrated in 2013, there is a both/and bipartisan option that could provide a pathway to citizenship combined with the paying of significant fines, which are a reasonable form of punishment (therefore, not amnesty) that avoid the deportation that is currently tearing many Latino families apart. Alas, hope for such a both/and approach assumes our elected politicians will embrace the conversational model for doing politics that I have proposed. (I am not holding my breath.)

The Colossian Forum

Before proceeding with my narrative, I need to dispel any false ideas that my approach to planting seeds of redemptive conversation is the only viable approach by focusing on similar work being done by The Colossian Forum (TCF).

During the early stages of my Respectful Conversation Project, I had the opportunity to meet with TCF President Michael Gulker and TCF Vice President Rob Barrett (a true kindred spirit), to talk about the significant similarities between my project and the work of TCF, which led to my service for a number of years as a TCF senior fellow.

As noted on their website, colossianforum.org, the mission of TCF is "to equip leaders to transform cultural conflicts into opportunities for spiritual growth and witness." TCF's vision is for "a Christian community that acts Christian, especially in the face of conflict."

The primary vehicle for TCF to provide hospitable spaces for conversation about divisive issues (my words for what TCF is doing) is through their excellent curricular program called The Colossian Way (TCW). This program features small-group face-to-face conversations in church settings. Curricular materials are currently available on the topics of origins, sexuality, and political talk. Whereas the goals of TCW and my Respectful Conversation Project are very similar, our respective pedagogies differ. Interested readers are encouraged to check out the details of the TCW program on the TCF website.

Called to Be Faithful, Not Necessarily Successful

By now you may be wondering about the extent to which I believe that my attempts to orchestrate respectful conversations will bear much fruit in an age characterized by vitriolic public discourse. I close this chapter with some reflections that I believe are relevant to that legitimate concern.

Christians have strong disagreements about the nature of the end times (eschatology). It is my understanding that the kingdom of God was inaugurated by the birth, life, and death of Jesus, but will only be fully realized some day in the future in ways that exceed my comprehension.

In the meantime, I believe that Christians are called to be agents for God's redemptive purposes, partnering with God, so to speak, by planting tiny seeds of redemption on earth (as we pray in the Lord's Prayer) that give intimations of the fully realized kingdom to come, analogous to the way in which an early morning sunrise hints at the eventual coming of the full noonday sun. The primary biblical teaching that informs this belief is the parable of the mustard seed told by Jesus, as recorded in Matthew 13:31–32:

> The kingdom of heaven is like a mustard seed that some-one took and sowed in his field; it is the smallest of all seeds, but when it has grown it is the greatest of shrubs and becomes a tree so that the birds of the air come and make nests in its branches.

It is this teaching that has kept me going in the midst of both the joys and pain I have experienced as I have aspired to be a faithful follower of Jesus.

The tiny seeds of redemption that I have focused on planting over many years have been seeds of redemptive conversation. It is important for me to reiterate the most fundamental premise underlying my planting of such tiny seeds—a premise that is my special response to the call of Jesus for all who claim to be his followers to love others: *to give someone who disagrees with you a safe and welcoming space to express that disagreement and then to talk respectfully about your disagreement is a deep expression of love.*

Recall my belief, learned mainly from my wife, Pat, that the primary motivation of love that informs my planting of seeds of redemptive conversation is a fruit of the Spirit that Christians are called upon to exemplify at all times, under any circumstances. In more academic language, this deep expression of love is an intrinsic value, important in and of itself, independent of whether it has the instrumental value of producing successful results.

That brings me to the question of whether my planting of seeds of redemptive conversation will prove to be successful. I believe that the modeling of respectful conversation that has been the focus of my Respectful Conversation Project has enjoyed some success in demonstrating that conversations among Christians having strong disagreements can be carried out with respect and can lead to uncovering areas of agreement and illuminating remaining areas of disagreement. But will my dream that this modeling will inspire others to do likewise be accomplished? I don't know. I can only envision that happening through the eyes of faith.

But I leave the issue of such broader success in God's hands. I am called to be faithful, not necessarily successful. I entrust to God the possible harvest from planting my tiny seeds of redemption. And as I trust God for that eventual harvest, I am encouraged by the reminder from John Howard Yoder that, all appearances to the contrary, the loving and nonviolent way of Jesus was indeed effective, but it calls for inordinate measures of faith, hope, and patience.

CHAPTER 8

Followers of Jesus Creating Inclusive Conversations within Churches

A s I gather with friends for coffee and cookies after the Sunday morning worship service at my home church, we often talk about the Cubs or the Twins (with me trying to slip in a few good words about my Cardinals) or the upcoming snowstorm or the latest happenings in our small town.

But we judiciously avoid talking about some hot-button issues about which we know there is significant disagreement within our diverse congregation—issues like same-sex marriage or political affiliation/engagement.

Of course, such lighthearted banter among friends is good. But it is problematic if at our church we never talk about our strong disagreements concerning difficult issues because we have embraced weak views of the Christian values of acceptance and peace instead of stronger views that have the potential to lead to deeper acceptance and more meaningful peace.

Weak and Strong Views of Acceptance and Peace.

I applaud those church congregations who have made a commitment to the core Christian value of acceptance. One such church that I know well has been criticized as the church where "anyone can go." That should be taken as a compliment. But I present two challenges for such churches.

First, it is too easy for the word "acceptance" to be interpreted in a very weak sense as mere tolerance. To illustrate this caution more concretely: a church may accept both gay and straight members and yet harbor sentiments among some of its members such as, "It is OK if those gay Christians worship with us, but once they are given positions of church leadership, I'm leaving for another church." (This is an actual quote from a member of a church that has admirably committed itself to the core value of acceptance.)

Secondly, it is too easy for a church that is committed to a core value of acceptance to interpret a related admirable commitment to the value of peace in the weak sense of absence of conflict, with the effect that those who worship at that church keep the peace by not talking to each other about their disagreements.

So while I applaud Christian churches that claim commitment to the Christian values of acceptance and peace, I want to challenge these gatherings of Christ-followers to aspire to stronger manifestations of acceptance and peace, as follows:

First, I believe that the word "acceptance" is too weak since it is too easily interpreted as only coexistence, sometimes in the extremely anemic sense of just putting up with someone. I prefer to think in terms of belonging.

As a Christian, I should help every other follower of Jesus in our group of believers to experience a strong sense of belonging. By this I mean that *"the other is received as one who is beloved."*[1] I should love everyone because everyone is loved by God. For example, I should start expressing my love for a married lesbian couple who attend my church by empathetically listening to their stories of the ways in which they have attempted to be followers of Jesus and the enormous obstacles they have faced during that quest.

Secondly, in a related way, all Christian churches need to move beyond a weak negative view of peace as absence of conflict to a strong view of peace as shalom: a state of affairs where everyone in the church community is flourishing in the midst of their diversity.

1. Dunn, *Romans 1–8,* 798; quoted by Wilson, *Letter to My Congregation,* 128 (emphasis original); drawing on Volf, *Exclusion,* 140–47.

Such flourishing precludes silencing anyone. Rather, it understands that we will flourish together only if we listen respectfully to each other's stories of the ways in which we aspire to be faithful followers of Jesus and the differing challenges that we have faced. In other words, we do not flourish when we suppress our disagreements. Rather, we flourish when we get our disagreements out on the table and talk respectfully about them, thereby opening up the possibility of learning from one another.

As you should expect by now, there is a fundamental premise that underlies my challenge to Christian churches to move from weak to strong views of acceptance and peace. All Christians agree that Jesus calls those who claim to be his followers to love others (Mark 12:31). But too many Christians ignore or violate a particular deep expression of such neighbor-love. As already stated, my fundamental premise is that *to create a safe and welcoming space for someone who disagrees with you to express that disagreement and to then talk respectfully about your disagreement is a deep expression of love.*

But how can Christian churches put into practice a commitment to strong views of acceptance and peace? Here is my proposal for your consideration.

Creating Flourishing Church Communities

What Should We Talk About?

Every church that I am familiar with has some type of mission statement that defines its purpose and ministry. Starting with such a statement, each church should critically examine itself to identify the main obstacles that hinder the full accomplishment of that mission. It should also seek to identify anything hindering full expression of a strong view of the Christian values of acceptance (viewing all members as belonging because they are beloved by God) and peace (collective flourishing).

After this initial stage of self-examination, each church should identify the issues that have emerged about which there is significant disagreement among members, placing these issues in priority order.

The church should then start with the top-priority issue, orchestrating respectful conversations, guided by the following recommendations.

Orchestrate One Initial Small-Group Conversation about the Top-Priority Contentious Issue

The strong versions of the Christian values of acceptance and peace that I now embrace call for the members of the church congregation to orchestrate a means for listening and talking respectfully to one another about their differing beliefs regarding the top-priority contentious issue that has been identified. Helping one another to experience a strong sense of belonging toward the goal of collective flourishing will continue to be impeded if we simply remain silent about our disagreements. We must talk to other members of our church about our disagreements, overcoming the fear that to do so may cause some in our church to leave for other churches where they can be sure to only hear echoes of their own beliefs.

But how should we talk to one another about contentious issues about which we have strong disagreements? I now propose concrete steps for orchestrating respectful conversations about any given contentious issue in Christian churches that reflect the lessons I have learned (some the hard way because of my past mistakes, as reported in chapter 7).

A Bad Place to Start

It is unwise to initiate a conversation about a contentious issue by inviting all members of a relatively large church to participate in a churchwide conversation.

There are two reasons why this is a bad place to start. First, a large-group conversation is not conducive to building the personal relationships of mutual understanding and trust that are foundational for eventually laying bare and sorting through disagreements.[2] That is because although members of a relatively large

2. The necessity of first "building personal relationships of mutual understanding and trust" before trying to discuss strong disagreements is well

church may think they know each other, it is generally not the case when it comes to addressing contentious issues. To get to know someone relative to a given contentious issue, you need to take the time to build a personal relationship of mutual understanding and trust by listening carefully to each person's position on the issue and his or her reasons for holding to that position in light of clearly stated value commitments. A large-group meeting is not conducive to this kind of careful listening to everyone's point of view.

Secondly, an open invitation to all members of a relatively large church may lead to an unbalanced cohort of those who accept the invitation that does not reflect the diversity in belief about the issue at hand that may exist within the church membership. If this happens, the ensuing conversation can deteriorate into an echo chamber where most attendees are exposed only to beliefs they already hold.

The Right Place to Start: Recruit a Small, Balanced Cohort of Conversation Partners

An appropriate leader in the church who knows its members well should identify two other community members to be co-planners. These should be members who are known to have significant disagreements about the issue at hand, but who also have exemplified that rare combination of commitment and openness that is an indispensable precondition for having a respectful conversation.

Each of these two co-planners should first recruit an appropriate number of other church members who they know generally share their respective beliefs about the issue at hand and who also have exemplified the requisite combination of commitment and openness. (For example, for a small group of eight conversation partners, each collaborator should recruit three other conversation partners.)

---

illustrated in my extended reports on how a Christian institution of higher education (Eastern University in Pennsylvania) and two churches (Sammamish Presbyterian Church in Washington and Zion Mennonite Church in Archbold, Ohio) engaged in challenging conversations about human sexuality issues in Heie, *Respectful LGBT Conversations,* 206–56.

There are two indispensable requirements when recruiting conversation partners. First, each of the co-planners should be sure to include members of the church whose lives are most affected by the issue at hand (e.g., a conversation about human sexuality should include gay Christians or a conversation about immigration should include immigrants, both documented and undocumented).

A second requirement when recruiting conversation partners is that the group should include persons who have proven expertise relative to the issue to be discussed. For example, a conversation about human sexuality should include persons who are conversant with the findings of scholars in various academic disciplines regarding same-sex attraction and sexual orientation. If the church has no such members, someone outside of the church membership should be invited to present such findings.

After recruiting conversation partners, the co-planners should choose a moderator for the upcoming small-group conversation, preferably a member of the given church. One criterion for selecting this moderator should be that while he or she may have a particular set of beliefs about the issue at hand, he or she is willing to hold those beliefs in abeyance during the conversation. He or she must take care to provide a safe and welcoming space for all points of view to gain a respectful hearing on an even playing field. Another criterion is that the moderator must be a good listener who has proven skills for being able to create safe and welcoming spaces for those who have strong disagreements to express and talk respectfully about those disagreements.

The co-planners should set the frequency of meetings (possibly one a month) and also select a venue for the upcoming conversation that they judge to be most appropriate given the circumstances (e.g., at the church, in a private home, or in a virtual venue like Zoom). The co-planners should be responsible for arranging the logistics for all of the meetings.

The First Session: Agreeing on the Purpose of the Conversation and Guidelines for Respectful Conversation

The stated purpose for the conversation should *not* be to win an argument. Rather, the purpose should be for each conversation partner to gain an adequate understanding of the views expressed by those partners who disagree with them, with a special focus on identifying the reasons they have for holding to a differing point of view in light of clearly stated value commitments. The goal is to identify areas of agreement and illuminate remaining areas of disagreement sufficient to enable ongoing conversation.

Based on my experience with my Trump conversation, reported in chapter 7, the "Guidelines for Respectful Conversation" to be agreed upon should be as follows:

- I will try to listen well, providing each person with a welcoming space to express her perspective on the issue at hand.

- I will seek to empathetically understand the reasons another person has for her perspective.

- I will express my perspective and my reasons for holding that perspective with clarity and conviction, but with a noncoercive style that invites conversation with a person who disagrees with me.

- In my conversation with a person who disagrees with me, I will explore whether we can find some common ground by critically examining my own view in light of her contrary view and the reasons she has for her view.

- Guided by the underlying values of humility, courage, patience, and love, when we cannot find common ground, I will always engage the person who disagrees with me in a way that demonstrates respect and concern for her well-being and does not foreclose the possibility of future conversations.

The Second Session: Getting to Know One Another

My experiences, both good and bad, in trying to orchestrate conversations among Christians having strong disagreements suggests that it is a big mistake to prematurely jump into laying bare the disagreements. A better strategy is to help the conversation partners get to know one another by starting with nonthreatening questions that call for descriptive rather than prescriptive responses.[3]

Therefore, my proposal for the second session is that each conversation partner should respond, without interruption, to the following questions:

- What elements of your personal story make this an important topic for you?

- What do you hope to get out of this conversation?

Preparation for the Third Session and Beyond: Deciding on Leading Questions

The purpose of the foundational work carried out in the first two sessions is to build personal relationships of mutual understanding and trust. It is only after this indispensable foundational work has been done that the conversation partners are adequately prepared to state their positions on the issue at hand and then to seek to identify areas of agreement and disagreement.

Whatever the issue at hand, careful steps need to be taken to formulate a series of leading questions that adequately address the various subtopics pertinent to that issue (as I did for my online conversation on human sexuality, as reported in chapter 7).

The two co-planners should provide leadership for this task. Their procedure for finalizing leading questions should strike a balance between taking into account questions that the conversation

---

3. An excellent example of this strategy is provided by Daniel Hill in his book *White Awake,* when he proposes that a good starting question for a conversation addressing the racial tensions that are currently prominent in America is "describe the first encounter you remember having with race" (47).

partners judge to be most pressing and advice from outside consultants as to the most important questions relative to the issue to be discussed. Some details for this procedure are as follows:

- Ask each conversation partner for input about what leading questions they consider to be most pressing.

- Seek consultation from a person or two (either within or outside the church membership) having expertise relative to the given issue as to the most appropriate leading questions. In particular, if scholars in the Christian academy have addressed aspects of the given issue, their advice should be sought.

To make these procedural recommendations more concrete, here is an example of what I judge to be some appropriate leading questions if the issue at hand is whether or not the church should provide temporary sanctuary for undocumented immigrants who have received deportation notices during that period of time when their cases are being lawfully adjudicated in court (a somewhat radical example, but one with which my home church has actually struggled).

- Is there a biblical mandate for churches to provide such sanctuary?

- What legal liabilities may a church face if it decides to provide sanctuary for undocumented immigrants?

- Is the church prepared to provide the services that would be needed by those residing on church grounds (possibly for an extended period of time)?

Based on this input regarding possible leading questions, the co-planners should decide on a final set of leading questions to be addressed, starting with the third session (taking as many sessions as are needed to adequately address these questions).

IDENTIFYING AREAS OF AGREEMENT AND DISAGREEMENT

I recommend that two sessions be devoted to each leading question. In the first session, each conversation partner should be given the opportunity to respond, without interruption, to the leading question, reading from a transcript that can be distributed to all the conversation partners shortly after this first session. The purpose of the transcript is to give each conversation partner time and a reference to seek to identify areas of agreements and disagreement in these various responses prior to the next session.

The second session for a given leading question should then be devoted to conversation about the various perceptions of areas of agreement and disagreement to see if any group consensus emerges.

Here are two suggestions about the best preparation for this second session. First, prior to this second session, it would be helpful for each conversation partner to send all the other conversation partners an email containing his or her perception of areas of agreement and disagreement.

A more radical idea for preparation for the second session is to encourage conversation partners to pair up prior to the second session to see if they can find areas of agreement that can be reported at the second session to get a headstart on seeing if the entire cohort shares those agreements. The logistical challenges to implementing this second suggestion will be formidable (getting very busy people together for one-on-one meetings in between full group meetings). But it may be worth an experimental try.

This succession of two sessions devoted to each leading question should be continued until all the leading questions have been addressed, at which time this initial small-group conversation will be completed.

Since the laying bare of agreements and disagreements, starting in the third session, must be preceded by the first two foundational sessions designed to build personal relationships of mutual understanding and trust, there should be no late entries to the cohort of conversation partners. Every conversation partner will be expected to attend each session, starting with the first session.

For the sake of informing possible follow-up small-group meetings or a larger community meeting (as discussed below) at the conclusion of this initial small-group conversation, each conversation partner should be asked to send the moderator his or her written responses to the following endgame questions:

- What areas of agreement, if any, emerged from this conversation?

- What major areas of disagreement still remain?

- What changes, if any, emerged in your beliefs about the issue we discussed as a result of our conversations?

- What changes, if any, emerged in your perceptions of those conversation partners who generally disagreed with you about the issue we discussed?

- Based on your experience in this conversation, what changes would you recommend for structuring possible future small-group conversations about this or other contentious issues?

Proceeding after This Initial Small-Group Conversation

How should a church proceed after concluding an initial small-group conversation about its top-priority contentious issue? There is no one simple answer to that question. Each church will have to answer that question based on its particular context and circumstances and its frank evaluation of the benefits reaped (or not) from its initial small-group conversation, as gleaned from the responses to the above endgame questions.

One option will be to initiate a number of additional small-group conversations to bring more members of the church into the conversation, possibly asking select conversation partners in this initial conversation to be moderators. This could be continued to eventually reach most, if not all, members of the church.

When, if at all, is a churchwide conversation called for? Again, I cannot generalize. As should be obvious by now, my preference is to conduct a series of small-group conversations since they are most conducive to building the requisite personal relationships of mutual understanding and trust needed as a foundation for talking respectfully about strong disagreements. But circumstances may suggest the need, eventually, for a conversation involving the entire church (e.g., if the church needs to make a churchwide policy decision regarding the issue at hand).

The Virulent Issue of Human Sexuality

The above set of recommendations to churches—starting with "What Should We Talk About?"—is intended to help individual churches foster respectful conversations about any contentious issue that is dividing the congregation. But I have found that if the contentious issue is human sexuality, navigating disagreements is notoriously difficult.

As I reported in chapter 7, my own attempt to orchestrate a small-group conversation on human sexuality issues proved to be a dismal failure, partly because I allowed late entries into the conversation who had not agreed to abide by the stipulated "Guidelines for Respectful Conversation" and hence did not consistently exhibit commitment to those guidelines after they entered the conversation. A proposal I will present below for navigating these troubled waters relative to human sexuality issues can remedy this gross deficiency. But I start with what I believe to be an enormous dilemma that is the main obstacle to ever creating a safe and welcoming space for LGBTQ Christians and straight Christians to gather in the same room together for respectful conversation (talking with each other rather than about each other).

On the one hand, many of our gay and lesbian brothers and sisters in Christ have suffered enormous pain when attempting to talk with other Christians who quickly tell them that they are "living in sin and on their way to hell." They have seldom, if ever, found a safe and welcoming space where they could tell their stories. In light of these painful experiences, why would they want to punish themselves further by entering the same room for conversation with those who have already consigned them to hell?

On the other hand, many Christians, myself included, have come to be advocates for our LGBTQ brothers and sisters in Christ only after getting to know them by means of authentic personal relationships—relationships predicated upon our willingness to get into the same room with them to listen to their personal stories of the challenges they have faced in their attempts to live faithful to their understanding of what it means to be a follower of Jesus.

So, how does one get beyond this dilemma? By expecting all the conversation partners to agree up front, before articulating their respective positions on the issue and sorting out their disagreements, to stipulated "Guidelines for Respectful Conversation" (such as those enumerated earlier in this chapter). I believe that if all the conversation partners would embrace these guidelines for conversation before expressing their positions, it is possible that they will all experience a safe and welcoming space to express their strong disagreements.

Of course, finding Christians on both sides of the contentious human sexuality issue who will be willing to embrace these "Guidelines for Respectful Conversation" will be a major challenge since, as I have suggested in chapter 6, you will need to identify Christians who embrace that extremely rare combination of deep commitment to their own beliefs and openness to carefully listening to and seriously considering the contrary positions of those who disagree with them, even allowing for the possibility that doing so may cause them to refine, or even correct, their present beliefs.

Extending to Church Denominations

My recommendations above for how individual church congregations should navigate contentious issues (human sexuality and otherwise) leaves open the question of how church denominations representing particular church traditions should struggle with contentious issues. That presents an enormous challenge. Since the human sexuality issue is particularly contentious, I will now limit myself to this issue in a way that I hope will be helpful to those many Christian traditions/denominations that have grappled with, or are currently grappling with, this issue, which has led to a number of denominational schisms, with more schisms likely to come.

For the interested reader, I have shared some reflections about how to navigate denominational conflicts regarding human sexuality in the book that emerged from my eCircle on that issue.[4] In those reflections, I appealed to the principle of subsidiarity, which holds that wherever possible, social and political issues should be dealt with at the local level.[5]

I herein reaffirm that subsidiarity principle in light of two foci in this book: the importance of first building personal relationships of mutual understanding and trust as a necessary foundation before attempting to uncover areas of agreement and disagreement, and the importance of giving a voice to everyone who will be affected by a decision. These two aspects of getting to know one another can best be accomplished at the local congregational level, rather than at a denominational level.

To make my subsidiarity position more concrete in a manner that is consistent with other emphases in this book, here are my reflections on the current human sexuality debate that is taking place in the denomination to which my church belongs, the Reformed Church in America (RCA).

Here is my summary of three scenarios that are currently being considered by a Vision 2020 team that was originally scheduled to report to the RCA General Synod meeting in June 2020 (which has been postponed due to the coronavirus pandemic):

- Scenario #1 (Staying Together): Keep the current RCA governance structure, but unify the RCA around a particular set of theological beliefs that allows for differing views on "all other questions."

- Scenario #2 (Radical Restructuring): Subdivide the RCA into three structures (mini-denominations) that provides room for theological diversity in light of differing views as to "priorities in mission" (apparently allowing for differing views about human sexuality).

4. Heie, *Respectful LGBT Conversations,* 273–79.
5. Heie, *Respectful LGBT Conversations,* 273.

- Scenario #3: (Grace-Filled Separation): Adopt one of three possible RCA-wide positions on human sexuality: a traditional view that reserves marriage for a man and a woman, a nontraditional view that allows for same-sex marriage, a "theologically moderate" view (what has been called a "third way"[6]) that allows for traditionalists and nontraditionalists to fellowship together "in tension" and then expecting that those congregations that do not agree with the adopted RCA-wide position will "leave the RCA graciously."

Consistent with my message in this book, I personally favor the first scenario, with the second scenario coming in second place (precluding the third scenario), for the following reasons.

The first scenario fits best with the existence of significant diversity in Christian beliefs, unified around a common commitment to be followers of Jesus, which, in my estimation, allows for disagreements about human sexuality issues. This reflects my belief that the question of whether God will bless a lifelong covenantal marriage commitment between same-sex partners is disputable, by which I mean that I know that there are deeply committed followers of Jesus who come out on different sides of that question.

Of course, since many members of RCA churches believe that the traditional view regarding human sexuality is indisputable, the challenge in trying to implement this first scenario will be to agree upon the particular set of theological beliefs about which all RCA churches must agree while allowing for disagreements about questions regarding human sexuality and other issues that are not deemed to be essential to RCA identity.

I view the second scenario as second best since it avoids yet another schism within the Christian church, which I believe is consistent with my desire to foster as much unity among followers of Jesus as is possible, given the reality of diversity in Christian beliefs. That is also my reason for precluding the third scenario.

---

6. For a splendid account of the challenges of forging such a third way, see Wilson, *Letter to My Congregation.*

Concluding Reflections on Christian
Higher Education

In this chapter, I have focused on providing practical advice about how to (and how not to) orchestrate respectful conversations about contentious issues in church settings. I believe that my recommendations can be adapted to Christian colleges and universities, although I will not attempt to do so here.

But what I will do is to outline why I believe such adaptation is sorely needed in Christian higher education, based on my bedrock premise, briefly noted in chapter 3, that the hallmark of higher education under Christian auspices should be *conversations seeking truth.*

To get beyond abstractions, I will set the stage by presenting what I have been told on good authority is the plight of LGBTQ students at one Christian liberal arts college (and, I suspect, many more).

At this one college, the LGBTQ students have been allowed to form a support group, but that group is not officially recognized by the college, one of the results being that they are not allowed to advertise their events on campus.

In effect, this group has been silenced, which, as this book seeks to make clear, is an unloving way to treat brothers and sisters in Christ. Why has this happened? Although the leadership at this school will hesitate to say this out loud, I have good reason to believe that at least one aspect of the rationale for such an unloving act is fear that if the constituents who support the college by sending their dollars and sons and daughters as students found out that these LGBTQ brothers and sisters in Christ were being given an equal voice, and were not being treated as second-class citizens in the campus community, many of them would withdraw their support.

If this rationale is operative, it explains an enormous existing obstacle to my ideal that the hallmark of Christian higher education ought to be "conversations seeking truth." There are obviously strong disagreements within this Christian community regarding human sexuality and same-sex relationships. But the message of this book is that such disagreements need to be out on the table, with everyone having an equal voice by being provided with a safe and welcoming space to state what he or she believes and his or her reasons for those beliefs, followed by respectful conversations that seek to sort through these disagreements.

As I have said, the practical recommendations provided in this chapter as to how churches should and should not orchestrate such respectful conversations can be adapted to Christian institutions of higher education. But the institution must first get beyond its fear and have the courage to commit itself to being a safe place for such conversations seeking truth to legitimately take place.

Back to the Fruit of the Spirit as Foundational

I close this book by coming full circle to the invaluable lesson that my wife, Pat, taught me many years ago. Relative to the foundational value question about what is important, I believe that what is most important for those of us who profess to be followers of Jesus is that we live true to a commitment to certain foundational Christian values, such as the fruit of the Spirit.

My experiences, good and bad, in trying to orchestrate small-group conversations among people who have significant disagreements suggest that conversation partners too often base their positions on a particular contentious issue on factors other than fundamental Christian values. In all the conversations that you have with other Christians about contentious issues, always encourage everyone to dig down deep to foundational Christian values.

And the Bible teaches that the most fundamental fruit of the Spirit is love. This book will make sense to you only if you share the fundamental premise that is the basis for all of it (which, for emphasis, I now state yet again): *to give someone who disagrees with you a safe and welcoming space to express that disagreement and then to talk respectfully about your disagreement is a deep expression of love.*

It is my hope and prayer that this book will challenge you to move beyond the current broken state of public discourse (within churches and everywhere else) by modeling in your daily life this loving way of respectfully engaging those who disagree with you.

ADDENDUM

Thank God for Your Mentors, and Thank Them, Too

In the main body of this book, I left out one of my most important mentors since the results of our engagement were not essential to my purposes for writing. But I add these reflections as an addendum because they bring home the point about how important it is to say thank you to your mentors.

Meet Forman Acton

It was a disappointing turn of events, or so it seemed at the time. My first two years of doctoral studies at Princeton were supported by a generous staff doctoral fellowship from my employer, the Hughes Aircraft Company. I needed continuing support. The options were a research fellowship, where you were paid to work on your doctoral dissertation (a nice deal) or a teaching assistantship, which typically meant grading homework or examinations for a professor (not such a nice deal—later in my teaching career, I jokingly said that I taught for nothing; I was being paid to grade).

I was given a teaching assistantship. During the second year, I was assigned to Forman Acton, a professor of electrical engineering, to assist him with a course in engineering mathematics. This unwanted assignment changed my life, since Forman was the best teacher I had ever encountered. His lectures were beautifully prepared and delivered with infectious enthusiasm. He exuded love for his subject matter and a deep concern for his students, including a strong commitment to helping them excel at learning.

I did some grading. But Forman also helped me spread my wings—like when he said to me one day, "Harold, I have to be away next Friday. Would you please teach my class for me?" Gulp! I did so, with much fear and trembling, preparing countless hours for a one-hour lecture. It went very well, and I loved it. Whereas I had enjoyed my work as an aerospace engineer, I now found something that I really loved to do. I realized I wanted to be like Forman.

To make a long story short, with one year left to work on my doctoral dissertation, I made a major career change at the tender age of twenty-seven. I did not return to the aerospace industry. Rather, I took a job teaching mathematics at The King's College (TKC), with an enormous cut in pay.[1]

During my seventeen years of teaching mathematics at TKC and Gordon College, I often told others (particularly the students I advised) about how the modeling provided by Forman Acton had inspired me to go into teaching. But I had never told the person who needed to hear this the most. So sometime during my twelfth or thirteenth year of teaching, I finally sent Forman a long hand-written letter, thanking him for his mentoring and inspiration.

I heard nothing back for quite a while. But I then received a long handwritten response, apologizing for the delay since he had been away from his office for the summer. He wrote, "I remember you, the blond kid with horn-rimmed glasses" (I would now settle for hair of any color). He went on to express his appreciation for my words of thanks.

I am glad that I finally took the initiative to thank Forman for his splendid mentoring. He passed away on February 18, 2004, at the age of ninety-three.

---

1. This decision was informed, at least in part, by advice the famous golfer Jack Nicklaus is reported to have given about choosing a vocation (I hope he said this, since I have been quoting him for years): "Find something you love to do so much that you would do it for nothing and then find someone who will pay you to do it."

Although not central to the purposes of this book, my regret for procrastinating in thanking Forman (repeating my regret in waiting seventy years to thank Pastor Omar) leads me to offer the following word of advice:

If you have not yet thanked someone who has served as a significant mentor in your life, please do so as soon as possible.

I recognize that not everyone has been as fortunate as I have to have splendid mentors who could expand my understanding of what it means to be a faithful follower of Jesus. In fact, some readers of this book may have had significant others in their lives who have been negative influences. If that has been your sad experience, or if you are simply interested in the possibility of two followers of Jesus learning from each other by talking about their differing pilgrimages, I offer the following suggestion:

Search out an acquaintance who you suspect, from a distance, has been earnest in seeking to faithfully follow Jesus and ask if you can just talk about anything that is on your mind and heart. My experience suggests that he or she will be delighted that you asked for such mentoring.

ADDENDUM

America after Donald Trump

I wrote this concluding addendum to my book in two parts. The first part, ending with the section "America after Donald Trump" was written on November 5, 2020, two days after Election Day, when the Associated Press declared that Joe Biden had defeated Donald Trump in the 2020 presidential election. As I wrote this first part, I assumed that the courts would not find sufficient merit in the lawsuits being filed in various states by Trump's lawyers to overturn this result (which proved to be the case). The second part of this addendum, titled "Democracy Wins: Hope for a Politics of Unity over Division," was written on January 10, 2021, ten days before Inauguration Day.

In the reflections that follow, I will first explain why I am pleased with this election result. I will then present my vision for the future of America, starting with the presidency of Joe Biden. A critical distinction that will inform all of my reflections is between the ends one hopes to accomplish through the political process (the goals of one's political agenda) and the political means one uses to accomplish one's desired ends. For reasons that will eventually become apparent, I start with the issue of means.

Contrasting Modes of Political Engagement

One important aspect of the means you choose to accomplish a desired political end is the manner in which you engage those who disagree with you about the desirability of that end.

It is a gross understatement to say that Donald Trump and Joe Biden take different approaches to engaging with those who disagree with them about the desirability of any given political end.

Donald Trump typically vilifies those who disagree with him by means of numerous tweets and interviews, often resorting to nasty name-calling and demonization. In doing so, he has played to the fears and resentments of his base and has sowed deep divisions among American citizens.

In stark contrast, Joe Biden's past political experience and his promise for the future point to his respect for those who disagree with him, which motivates his desire to build bipartisan bridges between those on opposite sides of the political aisle. (Whether Biden can succeed in building such bridges remains to be seen. More about that later.)

Why does this distinction in the means for engaging political opponents matter? Speaking first from my Christian perspective, it matters to me because Trump's manner of engagement is clearly antithetical to my understanding of the loving way in which Jesus calls Christians to engage those who disagree with them. As I have said many times in this book, I believe that a deep expression of loving one's neighbor, as we are called to do, is to create a safe and welcoming space for someone who disagrees with you to express that disagreement, followed by respectful conversation about the substance of the disagreement. I have seen absolutely no public evidence that President Trump ever practiced this deep expression of love of neighbor during his four years as our president.

Of course, not all Americans have made a commitment to the Christian faith. But it is my belief that this loving way of engaging those who disagree with you is an expression of our shared humanity, whatever religious or secular worldview one may be committed to.

But my concern about Donald Trump's vilification of those who disagree with him runs deeper than what I have just said. During the course of history, such vilification of political opponents has often been the first step away from democratic forms of governance to dictatorships. There is irrefutable evidence that Donald Trump has authoritarian, dictatorial tendencies that, if unchecked, could

lead to the unraveling of democracy in America.[1] (Witness his con-
tinuous assault on the checks and balances between the executive,
legislative, and judicial branches of government that our Founding
Fathers had the wisdom to establish.)

My primary reason for applauding the election of Joe Biden
is my rejection of the vitriolic means that Donald Trump uses to
engage those who disagree with him and my hope that the welcom-
ing-of-dissent approach that I believe Joe Biden will bring to his
presidential duties will preserve the messy democratic process of
doing politics in America.

But that conclusion on my part is based only on consideration
of the starkly contrasting means that Trump and Biden have chosen
to engage those who disagree with them. What about the political
ends that Biden will pursue and that Trump would have pursued
had he been reelected?

Consideration of contrasting political ends surely makes
things more complicated, as witnessed to by the fact that in the
local small-group conversation about the Trump presidency that
I recently hosted (reported on in chapter 7), all the conversation
partners agreed that the way in which President Trump engages
his political opponents does not measure up to their Christian
standards for lovingly engaging others. But, for the four Trump
supporters who participated in this conversation, this deficiency in
the means Trump has chosen to do politics is outweighed by the
political ends he has accomplished, which they view as being consistent with their Christian values. Therefore, I must now address
the thorny issue of the nature and significance of the contrasting
political ends embraced by Joe Biden and Donald Trump.

---

1. It is ironic and tragic that President Trump did not exercise his dictatorial tendencies when he should have right after the coronavirus arrived in
America. He should have made use of the Defense Production Act (DPA) to
mandate the production of needed medical supplies (e.g., Personal Protective
Equipment and ventilators) and he should have issued a national mandate for
the use of scientifically proven means for minimizing the spread of COVID-19
(e.g., the wearing of face masks and the practice of social distancing).

Contrary Beliefs about Political Ends

The substantive political issues about which Christians in America, and all other citizens, disagree are legion, including climate change, foreign trade policies, abortion, relationships with other countries, justice for all races and other people groups relative to opportunities and social benefits, and the list goes on.

To illustrate the complexity of the diversity of beliefs in our pluralistic society about any contentious issue, here are some snippets of the sharply contrasting beliefs about abortion that were expressed in the local small-group Trump conversation I recently hosted.

On the one hand, for one Trump supporter, a total ban on abortion at any time during a pregnancy was the only position consistent with biblical values. Therefore, her support of Trump in 2016 appeared to be based primarily on her belief that if Trump were elected president, he would advocate for the appointment of Supreme Court justices who would overturn Roe v. Wade and end the "abortion on demand" advocacy that she attributed to Hillary Clinton and, erroneously, to all Democrats.

In sharp contrast, other participants in the Trump conversation, including, but not limited to, Democrats, took a more nuanced position. While no participant embraced an "abortion on demand" position, some took the position that there may be tragic cases where an abortion is morally legitimate, such as a case where medical experts judge a choice must be made between saving the life of the mother and saving the life of the fetus. These dissenters to the "total ban on abortion" position also argued that a comprehensive and consistent pro-life position cannot limit itself to the single issue of protecting life before birth. Rather, attention must also be given to ensuring a high quality of life from the cradle to the grave.

In our Trump conversation, we did not resolve these stark disagreements about abortion. But we at least created a safe and welcoming space for these disagreements to be expressed and we got beyond the unloving tactic of vilifying those who disagreed with us. In fact, as reported in chapter 7, we came to acknowledge and respect the deep Christian commitment of those who disagreed with us about this hot-button issue, which was no small accomplishment.

So what is my point? My point, as you may guess from the rest of this book, is that the way to begin sorting through the starkly different beliefs that American citizens hold about desirable political ends is to create safe and welcoming spaces to talk respectfully to one another about our disagreements, with the hope that this arduous process will uncover some common ground. This utopian dream of mine certainly precludes the apparently automatic way in which Donald Trump immediately vilifies those who disagree with him and keeps alive my hope that the respectful way in which Joe Biden engages those who disagree with him will lead to a promising future for American democracy.

This concludes my major reasons for applauding the election of Joe Biden as our next president. But before proceeding with a possible cogent objection to what I have just said, I need to present two additional reasons I am pleased with the election of Joe Biden that focus on what I believe indisputable evidence suggests are two major flaws in both the character and presidential performance of Donald Trump that stand in stark contrast with Joe Biden.[2]

First, I believe that President Trump has exhibited extreme incompetence in his exercise of presidential duties, especially in his handling of the coronavirus pandemic.

There is irrefutable evidence, in his own words to Bob Woodward, that President Trump was aware of the seriousness of the coronavirus pandemic shortly after it entered the US, and he chose to downplay the threat rather than to vigorously address it. The result of such incompetence has been a staggering number of deaths, a significant percentage of which could have been avoided had Trump taken appropriate action recommended by public health officials to contain the spread of the virus.

Secondly, I believe that President Trump has exhibited a major character flaw in his inability to be truthful. On a personal level, I find this character flaw to be particularly troublesome because the primary value that has motivated my work over many years as a Christian educator has been the quest for truth.

---

2. For reflections from thirty evangelical Christians on the presidency of Donald Trump, see Sider, *Spiritual Danger of Donald Trump*.

The documented lies that Trump has told are legion. The most egregious recent lie has been his assertion that the virus is disappearing at a time when all the evidence pointed to the opposite—an increase in the number of hospitalizations and deaths. The magnitude and destructiveness of this lie are astonishing.

Of course, the question remains as to whether President Biden will do better relative to these two problems with the Trump presidency. I am optimistic for two reasons. Despite an occasional gaffe or two in his public statements, Biden is committed to telling the truth and when he discovers that he is wrong, he, unlike Trump, is willing to admit his error and adjust accordingly.

Relative to competence, I perceive a major contrast. Donald Trump has suggested that he "knows everything about everything" (my paraphrase of his exact words), and therefore, the legislative branch of government should just do what he thinks needs to be done. In stark contrast, Joe Biden gives evidence of commitment to the collaborative form of leadership that I believe is the most effective (see chapter 5)—leadership characterized by a willingness to learn from others and work together with others in a way that leads to some common ground that reflects the best insights and gifts of everyone.

A Major Objection: The Political Ends That President Trump Has Accomplished Comport with Christian Values

As already noted, the Trump supporters in my Trump conversation agreed that the way in which President Trump vilifies those who disagree with him is antithetical to Christian beliefs. Yet they support him. Why? Because they believe that what he has accomplished is consistent with Christian beliefs and priority must be given to those accomplishments.

Using the distinction between means and ends, the argument of these Christian supporters of Trump is essentially that the means that Trump has used, even if antithetical to the Christian faith, can be justified because of the good ends, from a Christian perspective, that these means have accomplished. This presents a major objection to my claim above that the unchristian manner in which Trump vilifies those who disagree with him (one aspect of his chosen political means) excludes supporting him, however much one may argue that the ends that he has accomplished are good in light of Christian values.

To make this more concrete, introducing the distinction between "good" and "evil," consider the argument that these Trump supporters make relative to "abortion on demand." They consider abortion on demand to be an evil that must be overcome. And overcoming this evil must take priority even if the means for doing so requires using another form of evil—the vilifying of political opponents.

Of course, this then raises the crucial prior question of whether a good end (from a Christian perspective) ever justifies an evil means (from a Christian perspective). The answer I find in Scripture is *no*.

Consider Romans 12:21: "Do not be overcome by evil, but *overcome evil with good*" (emphasis mine). This exhortation seems totally unrealistic, even outrageous. But that is what this passage of Scripture teaches.

I can anticipate the following response to this biblical teaching: trying to overcome the evil in America by "doing good" will not work. We Christians must protect Christianity in America from evil by whatever means we think will work.

My response centers on the words "protect Christianity." Are you suggesting God needs Donald Trump to protect Christianity in America? May I be so bold as to suggest that if you say that phrase to yourself over and over again, you will eventually see how ludicrous it is. Is your God so small that God must resort to using Donald Trump to protect Christianity in America?

Another way to look at this response is to return to a meddlesome section in chapter 5 where I call into question the tendency of many Christians to seek power within American culture. Christians who seek such power must give serious consideration to the response that Jesus gave to the temptation the devil presented to him in the wilderness, as recorded in Matthew 4:8–10:

> The devil took him to a very high mountain and showed
> him all the kingdoms of the world and the glory of them;
> and he said to him, "All these I will give to you if you
> will fall down and worship me." Then Jesus said to him,
> "Begone, Satan, for it is written, 'You shall worship the
> Lord your God and only him shall you serve.'"

Jesus rejected an amazing offer of power, opting for a different kind of power, the power of love.

America after Donald Trump

It is the power of love that animates my hope for the future of America after Donald Trump.

I see glimpses of the power of love in the self-sacrificing service provided in response to the coronavirus pandemic: the services of frontline doctors and nurses, often provided at great personal risk; the services of first responders, like EMT workers and fire fighters; and the services of essential workers, like those driving delivery trucks and stocking the shelves of grocery stores. I see it in the numerous little acts of kindness, like singing to neighbors from balconies and holding signs expressing love to those behind closed windows in nursing homes.

But it is difficult to detect examples of the power of love in the hyper-partisan, polarized world of American politics. The vilification of political opponents perpetuated by President Trump and his loyalists in the executive branch of government is the opposite of love.

How should Christians respond to this current brokenness in American politics? As I proposed in chapter 4, three responses are possible: domination, withdrawal, and conversation. Recall my rejection of the domination strategy since our Founding Fathers had the wisdom to establish a form of governance where proponents of diverse worldview beliefs, religious or secular, have an equal voice in legislating the laws of the land.

I must acknowledge that the current hyper-partisan, polarized, dysfunctional nature of current American politics makes withdrawal from politics a tempting option for Christians and all other American citizens. But I reject this option for Christians because of my deep conviction that God wishes to redeem all dimensions of life here on earth, including the apparently irredeemable realm of politics.

This leaves me with the conversation model for doing politics that I proposed in chapter 4. Recall that the basis for my proposing this model is my commitment to a number of Christian values. Love is foremost, but these Christian values also include humility, courage, respect, truth, justice, patience, and hope. And my proposal for political discourse in the political realm included the following three exhortations:

- Develop personal relationships of mutual understanding and trust with those with whom you have political disagreements.

- Listen carefully to those who disagree with you about political issues (as a deep expression of love) and, when you adequately understand their reasons for their positions, engage them in respectful conversation about your agreements and disagreements toward the goal of finding some common ground and illuminating remaining disagreements.

- Reach across the political aisle or dining room table to seek both/and positions that reflect the best insights of those on both sides of the aisle or table.

A common theme in these three exhortations is the need for bipartisanship in doing politics, with bipartisanship defined not in terms of the legislative result of political deliberation, but in terms of a practice; the practice of conversation where politicians on both sides of the political aisle seek common ground in the midst of their disagreements by means of respectful conversation characterized by exemplification of that rare combination of commitment to one's own beliefs and openness to carefully considering the contrary beliefs of others.

A focus on fostering such bipartisanship has been at the forefront of my personal political endeavors since 2008. And as you will soon see, it is the centerpiece of my vision for a political future for America after Donald Trump.

It was in the summer of 2008 that I agreed to serve as a local precinct captain for the presidential campaign of Barack Obama.[3] I assumed this responsibility because of Obama's stated commitment to take a bipartisan approach to doing politics.

How well did Obama live up to his promise of a bipartisan approach to doing politics? The results were mixed. My perception is the main reason for these mixed results was the intransigence of a highly polarized and hyper-partisan Congress.[4]

Despite the mixed results of President Obama's attempts to be bipartisan, my hope for the political future of America is that President Biden will experience some significant success at bipartisanship.

But Biden can't make bipartisanship in politics happen all by himself. He made this abundantly clear in his president-elect acceptance speech on November 7. In stark contrast to the *I* talk that permeated President Trump's pronouncements over the past four years, Biden focused on *we* talk: "We have to do this together"—a clarion call for bipartisanship in politics.

The monumental task facing President Biden includes *both* listening to *and* learning from the best insights of those Democrats

3. A major portion of my responsibilities as a local precinct captain was to canvas local neighborhoods, knocking on doors to advocate for candidate Obama. I did that for about three to four hours each Saturday for about eight weeks. Being an introvert by nature, I didn't look forward to these Saturdays. But in general, I was pleasantly surprised by what happened. Most notably, I discovered that a number of residents of Sioux County who invited me into their homes were polite and open to listening to my pitch for Obama (some of them even confessed to being closet supporters of Obama—feeling the need to stay in the closet because of the ultra-conservative nature of Sioux County, a county that was reported at the time to be the second most politically conservative county in America). The one exception to this generally good canvasing experience came when a resident of Rock Valley ran me off his lawn. Fortunately, I could run faster than him.

4. One example of such intransigence was the failure of Congress to take legislative action relative to the status of DACA recipients, known as Dreamers, which led Obama to take a much disputed executive action to allow undocumented immigrants who came to America as children to stay.

who are left of him on the political spectrum (e.g., Bernie Sanders) *and* those Democrats and Republicans who are right of him on that spectrum.

But is there a Christian basis for promoting bipartisanship? Absolutely! Here is where a Christian vision stands in stark contrast to the hyper-individualism that is so prominent in American culture. When the apostle Paul calls on Christians to emulate Jesus, as recorded in Philippians 2:4, he says, "Let each of you look not only to his own interests, but also to the interests of others." That is *we* talk, not *I* talk.

Since President Trump has sown fears, divisions, and animosities that feed on *I* talk and will not be easily healed, my dream of bipartisanship seems like utopian wishful thinking—an ideal that is beyond the real world of polarized American politics. It would surely be a remarkable exemplification of the power of love. I can only envision it happening through the eyes of faith.

Democracy Wins: Hope for a Politics of Unity over Division

America's Founding Fathers had the wisdom to set up checks and balances between the three branches of government: the executive, the legislative, and the judicial. This balance of powers has served our country well over most of our history. But it came under severe assault when President Donald Trump made decisions as if he had unlimited power to do as he pleased to satisfy his own self-interests. At the same time, with few exceptions, a hyper-partisanship has flourished in the halls of Congress that has led to legislative gridlock. The result has been a frontal attack on the checks and balances needed to maintain a robust democracy that would have been fatal to the American democratic experiment had it not been for the courageous public service of members of the judiciary from both sides of the political aisle who would not cave to the autocratic commitments of President Trump. Their meticulous commitment to the state and local laws governing election returns revealed the nonsense of President Trump's claims of widespread election fraud.

Although they were true to their callings as public servants who seek no recognition for doing their jobs, they are heroes who deserve our applause.

This victory for democracy has a deeper dimension upon which we need to focus. It points to the possibility of a return to a way of doing politics that is centered on building unity rather than creating self-serving divisions.

I believe it is fair to judge that President Trump's way of doing politics focused on creating divisions. Consider, for example, President Trump's approach to *not* addressing the rampant racial inequities in America. From the earliest days of his presidency when he declared that there were "good people on both sides" of the protests in Charlottesville, he has played to the fears of white Americans that people of color will erode their white privilege, thus creating unbridgeable divisions between white Americans and Americans of color. In the process of doing so, he has created a stark asymmetry between how differing groups of Americans view constitutionally permitted protests over racial inequalities: Black Lives Matter protestors are viewed by a significant group of Americans as inciters of violence, while those who oppose the Black Lives Matter movement are viewed as "peaceful protestors," with the result that nothing is done to address existing rampant racial inequalities.

This stark division that President Trump has sown is but one exemplification of the deeper problem with public discourse in America: tribalism, an us-versus-them mentality that holds that "those other folks" not only lack any understanding of the "truth" about the contentious issue at hand, they are also downright evil and need to be demonized. Such tribalism is the inevitable result of the politics of division that has been consistently practiced by President Trump.

But I close these reflections with two rays of hope. First, President-Elect Biden has pledged to replace a politics of division with a politics of unity—not unity in always forging agreement as to legislative results, but unity in sharing a commitment to the bipartisan practice of respectful conversation about disagreements. Of course, time will tell whether that is possible.

My second ray of hope is that out of the current political chaos a new vision for the Republican Party will emerge that will reject the present Trump version, returning in some form to the meaning of Republicanism that characterized the Reagan era. In his splendid book, *We Should Have Seen It Coming*,[5] Gerald F. Seib notes the following three elements of Reaganesque Republicanism: limited government characterized by fiscal responsibility, welcoming of the immigrant, and a foreign policy that promotes democracy around the world. All three of these emphases have been rejected by the present Trump version of Republicanism. It is my hope that, in place of Trumpism, a group of Republican legislators will shape a new form of Republicanism that embraces these commitments. The most likely current Republican legislators who could focus on this task could include Mitt Romney (Utah), Susan Collins (Maine), Ben Sasse (Nebraska), Liz Cheney (Wyoming), Adam Kinzinger (Illinois), and Lisa Murkowski (Alaska).

5. Seib, *We Should Have Seen It Coming*.

Afterword

As I write, it is eight days before the 2020 elections in the United States. When you read this, the outcome of those elections will be long established (one dares to hope). But the brutal divisions that accompanied the election season will not have magically healed.

A story. In my extended family, a member of the twenty-something generation communicated online to his mother that her pending vote for Donald Trump means that she is "crazy," "racist," and "evil." He went on to say that his (future) children can have nothing to do with her. I happen to know that the recipient of this communication is not crazy, racist, or evil. But her vote is understood by this young man to represent a total endorsement of the character of Donald Trump—indeed, a total immersion in that character. The concept that her vote—with which I certainly do not agree—need not be interpreted as a moral endorsement/collapse seems lost on this young man. And so, yet another bond breaks in American life—this time between a mother and her son—over an ephemeral political difference of opinion.

The year began with the *Atlantic* doing a cover package on the possibility of civil war in America. The year continued with street protests over the George Floyd murder, some rioting, and then waves of heavily armed counterprotesters looking for trouble, and sometimes finding it. Black Lives Matter vs. Proud Boys is a microcosm of a society ripping apart at the seams. It seems to me that only COVID has spared us a summer and fall filled with more such confrontations all across America.

Afterword

Harold Heie has spent decades doing the hard work of advancing respectful conversations across various stark divides. He understands what is at stake, what approaches have the best chance of working, and what spirit is required to keep relationships alive even when they are strained by convictional differences. This book embodies some of the most important lessons that he has learned along the way. I consider it essential reading.

Sometimes it seems that we can live in peace with others in this society only if we routinely bite our tongues and bury our core convictions. But because our convictions tend to ooze out anyway, this strategy most often fails. On the other hand, sometimes we and others seem to act as if daily confrontation with those evildoers who don't see the world the way we do is what conscience requires. But this leads to a lifestyle of constant, grinding conflict—or worse.

Neither approach seems to reflect the way of Jesus or the best of the Christian tradition. Jesus never seemed to bite his tongue or bury his core convictions. But neither did he appear to be looking for a fight. He spoke the truth in love. We lack Jesus's perfect knowledge or perfect love. We need the humility of openness to learn from others, even those with whom we disagree. We need to value relationships enough to hang in there in conversation even when it is excruciating. And we need to learn the skills of civil, respectful dialogue that Harold Heie teaches so aptly.

With even churches splitting apart on left/right lines, Harold Heie's project seems more important than ever. May his tribe increase.

David P. Gushee

Afterword: For Such a Time as This

Given what we've just read, the last thing we need is a word from me. And maybe that's particularly true for the author, since I've participated in a few of his lows (and Heies) over the years. But the truth is, Harold has lived the truth of which he speaks. Not easily. Not without paying a price which has been burdensome to his heart as well as his head. But it has been a consistent theme modeled in good times as well as bad.

We became friends during the early years in our scholarly careers, even though he came out of the world of math and I was a mere sociologist. Oddly, both of us loved philosophy as well, which helped bridge our differences. Plus, we wound up on a campus with folks like James Skillen and Malcolm Reid, who encouraged us to think beyond the borders and particularly to ponder the ontological roots of our musings. In my case, at least, it was quite transformative. And without a doubt, Harold was part of that transformation.

In not too long, however, everything started going downhill. We both slid into administrative posts, which eventually took us to different campuses and deprived me of ongoing conversations that I deeply valued. But something else happened as well, which is a little more difficult to explain. Nevertheless, over time, we started to disagree on some of the implications of the deeper truths we both embraced. This was difficult, in part, because we are both a tad inner-directed (in the David Riesman sense of the term) and quite confident of our various conclusions. But more importantly, these differing assessments carried significant implications not only for the work we were doing, but also for the schools, churches, and communities we were serving. Plus, we were living in a polarized culture, which has only grown more divided over the years.

But here's the deal: Harold neither flinched from the truth he affirmed nor from the determination to discern the other side. To speak as well as listen. To share and also learn. It's precisely what he is calling for in this book, of course, but he put it into practice long before he had any intention of writing such a thing. And what has been the result? A career that did not reach its summit through positions or typical biographical accomplishments, though there were many of those; instead, he pursued an intentional strategy to bring brothers and sisters together to actually *be* a family, sometimes through planned conferences and dialogues, which have become legendary, but also through daily conversations with those the Lord has given him, wherever he has journeyed.

Which means, if you want to see what this book looks like, lived out in everyday life, then fix your eyes on the author who, for starters, never diminished me because of my contrary thoughts or lack of imagination. At the same time, he never allowed my errors to go unattended nor refused to discern a better way forward when such a thing was possible. For that reason, Harold Heie has not only become my teacher, but my exemplar. It's a much-needed gift at such a time as this. Thanks be to God.

Stan D. Gaede

About the Authors

HAROLD HEIE served as founding director of the Center for Christian Studies (now the Center for Faith and Inquiry) at Gordon College and as vice president for academic affairs at both Messiah College and Northwestern College (Iowa), after teaching mathematics at Gordon College and The King's College. He holds a PhD in aerospace sciences from Princeton University and served as a trustee of the Center for Public Justice, as a senior fellow at the Council for Christian Colleges and Universities (CCCU), and as a senior fellow at The Colossian Forum. He also served as co-director of CASA of Sioux County (Center for Assistance, Service, and Advocacy), a nonprofit devoted to welcoming, empowering, and celebrating people from all cultures, with a special focus on helping Latino community members to flourish.

In 2011, Heie founded the Respectful Conversation Project on his website, respectfulconversation.net, which is devoted to encouraging and modeling respectful conversations among Christians who have strong disagreements about contentious issues. His website has hosted four major electronic conversations (eCircles), the highlights of which have been reported in the following four books: *Evangelicals on Public Policy Issues: Sustaining a Respectful Political Conversation* (2014); *A Future for American Evangelicalism: Commitment, Openness, and Conversation* (2015); *Respectful LGBT Conversations: Seeking Truth, Giving Love, and Modeling Christian Unity* (2018); and *Reforming American Politics: A Christian Perspective on Moving Past Conflict to Conversation* (2019).

RICHARD J. MOUW was president of Fuller Theological Seminary from 1993 through June 2013, and presently serves as a senior research fellow at the Henry Institute for the Study of Religion and Politics at Calvin College. Prior to joining the Fuller faculty in 1985, he taught in the philosophy department at Calvin College (now Calvin University). Mouw has also served as visiting professor at several institutions, including the Free University in Amsterdam.

A graduate of Houghton College, Mouw studied at Western Theological Seminary and earned a master's degree in philosophy at the University of Alberta. His PhD in philosophy is from the University of Chicago. Mouw is the author of twenty books and has received several awards, including Princeton Theological Seminary's 2007 Kuyper Prize for Excellence in Reformed Theology and Public Life, and the Shalom Award for Interfaith Cooperation from the American Jewish Committee. He served as president of the Association of Theological Schools and co-chaired the official Reformed-Catholic Dialogue for six years.

DAVID P. GUSHEE (PhD, Union Seminary, New York) is distinguished university professor of Christian ethics and director of the Center for Theology and Public Life at Mercer University.

Gushee is the former president of both the American Academy of Religion and the Society of Christian Ethics, signaling his role as one of the world's leading Christian scholars. He is (co)author and/or (co)editor of twenty-five books, which together have sold more than 100,000 copies and been translated into a dozen languages. His most recognized works include *Righteous Gentiles of the Holocaust*, *Kingdom Ethics*, *The Sacredness of Human Life*, and *Changing Our Mind*. His new book, *After Evangelicalism*, charts a theological and ethical course for postevangelical Christians. As of this writing, it is the #1 new release in three different Amazon.com categories.

Gushee has also published more than 150 academic book chapters, journal articles, and reviews. An award-winning teacher, he offers courses both to seminarians and college students. During a distinguished twenty-seven-year career, he has written hundreds of opinion pieces, given interviews to scores of media outlets, and has led significant activist efforts on climate, torture, and LGBTQ inclusion.

About the Authors

S TAN D. GAEDE has served as president of both the Christian College Consortium and Westmont College, and as provost at both Gordon College and Westmont. After earning a BA at Westmont College and a PhD in sociology at Vanderbilt University, he served on the faculty at Gordon College for over two decades. In that role, he also served as an undergraduate mentor to two of the most distinguished Christian sociologists of our day: James Davidson Hunter of the University of Virginia and Christian Smith of the University of Notre Dame.

Stan Gaede has written seven books, including *When Tolerance Is No Virtue* and *An Incomplete Guide to the Rest of Your Life*. He received the Alumnus of the Year award from Westmont College in 2012, and was given the Distinguished Faculty Award at Gordon in 1982, 1987, and 1992. A frequent commencement speaker and lecturer in the Christian liberal arts, he was honored in 2006 when Westmont College dedicated the Gaede Institute for the Liberal Arts.

Bibliography

Barbour, Ian. *Myths, Models, and Paradigms: A Comparative Study in Science and Religion.* New York: Harper & Row, 1974.

Biggar, Nigel. *Behaving in Public: How to Do Christian Ethics.* Grand Rapids: Eerdmans, 2011.

Brekus, Catherine A., and W. Clark Gilpin. *American Christianities: A History of Dominance and Diversity.* Chapel Hill: University of North Carolina Press, 2011.

Brooks, Arthur C. *Love Your Enemies: How Decent People Can Save America from the Culture of Contempt.* New York: Broadside, 2019.

Browning, Robert. "My Star." https://www.poetryfoundation.org/poems/43769/my-star.

Clouser, Roy A. *The Myth of Religious Neutrality: An Essay on the Hidden Role of Religious Belief in Theories.* Notre Dame, IN: University of Notre Dame Press, 2005.

Dunn, James D. G. *Romans 1–8.* Word Biblical Commentary 38A. Nashville: Thomas Nelson, 1988.

Evans, Christopher H. *Histories of American Christianity: An Introduction.* Waco, TX: Baylor University Press, 2013.

Fea, John. *Was America Founded as a Christian Nation?: A Historical Introduction.* Louisville: Westminster John Knox, 2016.

Fletcher, Joseph. *Situation Ethics: The New Morality.* Library of Theological Ethics. Louisville: Westminster John Knox, 1966.

French, David. *Divided We Fall: America's Secession Threat and How to Restore Our Nation.* New York: St. Martin's, 2020.

Goleman, Daniel. "Leadership That Gets Results." *Harvard Business Review,* Mar.–Apr. 2000. https://hbr.org/2000/03/leadership-that-gets-results.

Heie, Harold. "Dialogic Discourse: Christian Scholars Engaging the Larger Academy." *Christian Scholar's Review* (Spring 2008) 347–56.

———. *Evangelicals on Public Policy Issues: Sustaining a Respectful Political Conversation.* Abilene, TX: Abilene Christian University Press, 2014.

———. *A Future for American Evangelicalism: Commitment, Openness, and Conversation.* Eugene, OR: Wipf & Stock, 2015.

Bibliography

————. *Learning to Listen, Ready to Talk: A Pilgrimage toward Peacemaking.* New York: iUniverse, 2007.

————. "Mathematics: Freedom within Bounds." In *The Reality of Christian Learning: Strategies for Faith-Discipline Integration,* edited by Harold Heie and David L. Wolfe, 206–30. Grand Rapids: Eerdmans, 1987.

————. *Reforming American Politics: A Christian Perspective on Moving Past Conflict to Conversation.* Canton, MI: Front Edge, 2019.

————. *Respectful LGBT Conversations: Seeking Truth, Giving Love, and Modeling Christian Unity.* Eugene, OR: Cascade, 2018.

Hildreth, Matthew. "'White, Conservative, and Dumb'—and Other Lies about Rural America." *Sojourners* (June 2020) 24–29. https://sojo.net/magazine/june-2020/white-conservative-and-dumb-and-other-lies-about-rural-america.

Hill, Daniel. *White Awake: An Honest Look at What It Means to Be White.* Downers Grove, IL: InterVarsity, 2017.

Holmes, Arthur. *All Truth Is God's Truth.* Grand Rapids: Eerdmans, 1977.

————. *The Idea of a Christian College.* Grand Rapids: Eerdmans, 1975.

Jacobsen, Douglas, and Rhonda Hustedt Jacobsen. *Scholarship and Christian Faith: Enlarging the Conversation.* New York: Oxford University Press, 2004.

Junger, Sebastian. *Tribe: On Homecoming and Belonging.* New York: Hachette, 2016.

Lewis, C. S. *Reflections on the Psalms.* New York: Harcourt, Brace & World, 1958.

Mouw, Richard. *Uncommon Decency: Christian Civility in an Uncivil World.* Downers Grove, IL: InterVarsity, 2010.

Niebuhr, H. Richard. *Christ and Culture.* New York: Harper & Row, 1951.

Olson, Roger E. *Reformed and Always Reforming: The Postconservative Approach to Evangelical Theology.* Acadia Studies in Bible and Theology. Grand Rapids: Baker, 2007.

Ostrander, Rick. *Why College Matters to God.* Abilene, TX: Abilene Christian University Press, 2009.

Palmer, Parker J. *The Active Life: A Spirituality of Work, Creativity, and Caring.* New York: HarperCollins, 1991.

————. *The Courage to Teach: Exploring the Inner Landscape of a Teacher's Life.* New York: John Wiley, 2017.

————. *Healing the Heart of Democracy: The Courage to Create a Democracy Worthy of the Human Spirit.* San Francisco: Jossey-Bass, 2011.

————. *To Know as We Are Known: Education as a Spiritual Journey.* New York: HarperCollins, 1983.

Potok, Chaim. *The Chosen.* New York: Ballantine, 1996.

Schrock-Shenk, Carolyn. "Foreword." In *Stumbling toward a Genuine Conversation on Homosexuality,* edited by Michael A. King, 13–18. Living Issues Discussion 4. Telford, PA: Cascadia, 2007.

Seib, Gerald F. *We Should Have Seen It Coming: From Reagan to Trump—A Front Row Seat to a Political Revolution.* New York: Random House, 2020.

Bibliography

Sider, Ron, ed. *The Spiritual Danger of Donald Trump: Thirty Evangelical Christians on Justice, Truth, and Moral Integrity.* Eugene, OR: Cascade, 2020.

Smith, James K. A. *Desiring the Kingdom: Worship, Worldview, and Cultural Formation.* Grand Rapids: Baker Academic, 2009.

Wilson, Ken. *A Letter to My Congregation: An Evangelical Pastor's Path to Embracing People Who Are Gay, Lesbian, and Transgender into the Company of Jesus.* Canton, MI: Read the Spirit, 2014.

Wolterstorff, Nicholas. "Scholarship Grounded in Religion." In *Religion, Scholarship, and Higher Education: Perspectives, Models, and Future Prospects,* edited by Andrea Sterk, 3–15. Notre Dame, IN: University of Notre Dame Press, 2002.

Yoder, John Howard. *The Politics of Jesus.* Grand Rapids: Eerdmans, 1972.

———. *The Priestly Kingdom: Social Ethics as Gospel.* Notre Dame, IN: University of Notre Dame Press, 1984.

Zehr, Howard. *Changing Lenses: Restorative Justice for Our Times.* Harrisonburg, VA: Herald, 2015.